Breaking from Realism

A Map/Quest for the Next Generation

Anne~

Thank you for pointing
me in their direction long
ago!

Breaking from Realism

A Map/Quest for the Next Generation

by Michael Bigelow Dixon

Smith and Kraus Publishers

2014

Sections of this book are adapted from the following articles with permission of the co-authors and the Educational Theatre Association.

"Breaking with Realism: Playwriting for the 21st Century," by Michael Bigelow Dixon and Amy Wegener, *Teaching Theatre, vol. 22, No. 4*, Educational Theatre Association, Summer 2011.

"Expressionism and Alternate Worlds: Breaking with Realism Part II," by Michael Bigelow Dixon and Amy Wegener, *Teaching Theatre, vol. 23, No. 1*, Educational Theatre Association, Fall 2011.

"When Worlds Collide: Breaking with Realism Part III," by Michael Bigelow Dixon, *Teaching Theatre*, Educational Theatre Association, *vol. 23, No. 2*, Winter 2012.

"The Main Event: Breaking with Realism Part IV," by Michael Bigelow Dixon, *Teaching Theatre, vol. 23, No. 3*, Educational Theatre Association, Spring 2012.

"The Case Is Submitted: Re-enactment Theatre and U.S. Supreme Court Oral Arguments," by Michael Bigelow Dixon and Nina Kasniunas, *Teaching Theatre, vol. 21, no. 2*, Educational Theatre Association, Winter 2011.

And the Truth Serum Will Set You Free © Bevly Anderson

Four Measures © Tony Del Grosso

Odyssey Across America: a bricolage © Harold N. Cropp

Carrion (audio and graphic plays) © Val Smith

"Depth", "Movement", "Out of the Box" © DFK/Dixon Studios

A Better Door © George Brandt

The Weight © Susan Apker

Turning Away © Margaret Lynch

The Case Is Submitted: Boy Scouts of America, Monmouth Council v. Dale (adaptation) © Michael Bigelow Dixon

ISBN: 1575258684
ISBN: 9781575258683
Library of Congress Control Number: 2013957186

Typesetting, layout, by Elizabeth E. Monteleone
Cover Art: Bruce Holwerda

A Smith and Kraus book
177 Lyme Road, Hanover, NH 03755
editorial 603.643.6431 To Order 1.877.668.8680
www.smithandkraus.com

Sullivan Canaday White

"Friendship, not technology, is the only thing capable of showing us the enormity of the world."

– Steven Dietz

Acknowledgments

For their enthusiasm, generosity, and contributions to this book, I am deeply indebted to the following playwrights, artists, editors, professors, family members, and friends. Were it not for encouragement from Don Corathers, Jim Palmarini, and Julie York Coppens at the Educational Theatre Association I never would have assembled these workshop projects into a single volume. Don, Jim, and Julie made a sustained commitment to publishing these ideas in a series of articles, and then proved to be excellent editors, as well. Actors Theatre of Louisville Literary Director Amy Wegener helped launch the project at a Humana Festival "College Days" workshop and, as always, it was a joy to work with her as co-author on the first two articles in the series. I am beholden to Janet Keller and Valerie Smith at Janet Keller Editing for their intellectual prowess and editorial acuity. Via their impressive catalog, Marisa Smith and Eric Kraus have contributed greatly to the published resources and record of the American theatre, and their interest helped spur me on to complete this volume. Jessica Burgess at the Inkwell Theatre in Washington, D.C., took a chance and invited me to test these ideas with area playwrights, and Carter Lewis at Washington University was the first playwright/professor to request these workshop plans. As Chair of the Theatre Department at Goucher College, Allison Campbell gave me free range to experiment in class with these ideas. Professor/visual artist Cornell Rubino made the graphic play project a success, and Professor Nina Kasniunas added political science expertise to the Supreme Court Do-Over. An up-and-coming theatre artist, Kristen Noelle Ballard, provided invaluable research. Without their trust and permission, I would not have been able to include fascinating excerpts from new plays by Naomi Wallace and Arthur Kopit, which were unpublished manuscripts at the time. Eric Schmiedl graciously offered to lead a workshop with the talented members of the Cleveland Playwrights Unit, which resulted in the ekphrastic plays included in this book. Transylvania University art professor Jack Girard has been extremely supportive of my teaching and these workshops. Thank goodness for Transy playwriting students, who bolstered my confidence by demonstrating week after week that these exercises – some of which, it seemed to them, might have been conceived by Lewis Carroll – could bring out the best in their imaginative writing. Thanks Gub, Frank, Janet, Charlie, Hal, Adrienne, Amanda, Gregg, Gary, Julie, Kelly, Melodie, Yehuda, Dean, Cuzzie and Doc. And finally, for all the long conversations, endless encouragement, and real inspiration, I am most indebted to Sully White.

TABLE OF CONTENTS

TABLE OF PLAYWRIGHTS AND PLAYS

FOREWORD

The hardest thing for an actor, a director, or a teacher to do on this earth is to change. What? Give up our hard won expertise, our deeply defended comfort zone, the little space we've secured for our ego and venture *out there*? Huh-uh. Pull down the shades and pass the hot chocolate. And let's face it, all of us except Jimmy (poor old Jimmy) have been trained in the realist tradition by Konstantin, done our work in the realist tradition (of course we have no beef with direct address and the simplicity of the bare stage – we're flexible) and have lately been listening to David Mamet because, hey, we're ready to grow. But the real secret is that no one has explained in a non-threatening way what's out beyond some version of the kitchen sink. If the scene isn't basically linear and the storytelling wouldn't make Aristotle happy and it combines art forms and genres and split focus and technology, we know one thing and one thing only ... we have no idea how to do that and we are not going out on the dance floor and make fools of ourselves.

Enter Michael Dixon and this book. In clear, dexterous, inviting prose he invites us in to a new way of understanding the possible, undertaking the new, and experiencing an expanded theatrical universe. Like the old Fred Astaire Dance Studio's you can "walk in and dance out." The ideas, concepts, and possibilities Michael demystifies are already here, already vibrant, and this tsunami of information and image that defines the new modernism is going to sweep a lot of old orthodoxies right out of the room. Or, less cataclysmically, it's definitely going to be our roommate. Like Madam Arkardina in *The Seagull*, we're going to have to live with new forms, born in a new world and espoused by a new generation, so we old realists have the choice of obsolescence or rebirth.

Michael serves up a delicious feast of transformations and makes it impossible not to want to dig in or (to hopelessly mix the metaphor) at least to dip a toe in the water. This is a book without "isms", but it is the best of siren calls. Any teacher or practitioner should put this book where you can't get around it on your way to the refrigerator. It's going to make a lot of classrooms and productions a quest instead of an answer and won't that be ... well ... a relief?

—Jon Jory

Another requirement for the creative person which is even more difficult to accept: gullibility ... a willingness to explore everything: to be open, innocent and naïve before rejecting anything.

– Silvano Arieti, *The Magic Synthesis*

Begin by Ending

It is a symptom of the lost faith in theatre as an art form that its practitioners require the credentials of authenticity.

– Howard Barker, *Theatre without a Conscience*

I was leading a playwriting workshop in 2011 with 25 college students during the Humana Festival of New American Plays at Actors Theatre of Louisville, and I began by asking each of them to write a short scene that we would work with. They all wrote realistic scenes with recognizable locations, familiar characters, and predictable conflicts. All of them. And these were theatre students interested in new plays. An alarm went off in my head. Was realism their preferred style or was it a default mode? What was their theatrical experience and what were their influences? How is playwriting being taught to the next generation and does it steer young writers toward or away from the conventions of realism?

As a playwriting professor, I've used Jeffrey Hatcher's *The Art & Craft of Playwriting* and Stuart Spencer's *The Playwright's Guidebook* in my Introduction to Playwriting courses. Both books feature clear analysis and helpful explanations regarding basic elements of dramatic writing, such as action, conflict, plot, and character development. Both cite classic plays as examples. From these two authors – both of whom are accomplished playwrights – my students have learned how to structure action, locate the point of attack, raise stakes, and orchestrate character conflict.

Though my students learn the core principles of good playwriting, they apply them within the rather limited sphere of their own experience. College students have seen thousands of films and television dramas and comedies, 99.9 percent of which are locked into the conventions of realism. By the time they're twenty, students have internalized those conventions as standards for dramatic storytelling in any medium. So naturally they aspire to write excellent plays according to the rules of the art form as it is presented to them, mostly through media other than theatre.

There are, of course, plenty of non-realistic dramas being produced in the American theatre, but not so much in the mainstream – Broadway, commercial Broadway tours, regional theatres, and summer stock companies. Most of the non-realistic work happens, as it has over the past 125 years, in small spaces, generally downtown, and in productions considered experimental by most audiences and critics. The truth is, however, not many students see those productions. Instead, they work under the influence of mainstream realism and they write realistic plays, which, if they're good, reinforce realism as a standard for their continued writing and for the students who follow. This cycle of formula and imitation seriously limits the potential for discovering new ways of writing and new ways of thinking about what theatre is, or could be.

With this book I want to do something that will help students break from an almost unquestioned allegiance to the tenets of realism in order to explore a wider world of theatrical possibilities. In the American arts, the idea of creativity focuses mostly on *how* things are done rather than *what* is done. The *what* – the object, the subject, the idea, or the thing – is most often familiar. Occasionally there's a breakthrough – a new *what* is invented, discovered, theorized, or imagined – but mostly artists work within or against the known. This is especially true in drama, the subject of which is human experience. Though the trappings have changed over time, the essential dilemmas confronting or caused by people remain the same. That's why we can relate to characters in plays two thousand years old. It's *how* characters in such dilemmas are depicted that reveals a playwright's creative and imaginative powers.

When the *how* doesn't evolve or is locked into stage conventions that have become tired or stale, playwrights and their art form suffer. This is what happened with realism in its more extreme form – naturalism. In *Great Reckonings in Little Rooms*, Bert O. States writes:

> I say there was a crisis of self-perfection not because the world was tiring of Ibsen and Chekhov, or because there was no social work left for naturalism to do, but because there was nothing *new* it could do, as a mature style, without repeating itself to death.

That now describes the trajectory of realism in the 21st century.

So, this book is all about *how*. *How* to guide playwrights away from conventions they accept as the foundation of storytelling on stage? *How* to help them develop their "voices" in forms of theatre that currently don't exist – forms they'll need to discover or invent? *How* to encourage them to experiment with conventions rather than adhere to them, especially when experimentation takes time and may appear to result in nothing productive. Of course, there is another way to think of time spent on research and development. After years of testing every conceivable variation of a light bulb, Thomas Edison acknowledged, "I have not failed. I've just found 10,000 ways that won't work." And then, of course, he found a way that did.

These are the questions that lead to the creative method outlined here, a method that focuses primarily on process, form, and diverse ways of thinking about a dramatic event. To take you into the realm of non-realism in what follows, I offer a brief history of theatrical conventions situating the challenge of transcending realist conventions for the American stage in its past. I then summarize 15 novel strategies for composition thereby launching the presentation of workshops in creative methods.

The basic lessons taught by Hatcher, Spencer, and others are indispensible to good dramatic writing. However, young playwrights must also realize that, just as subject matter is a choice, so is form. Moreover, the exploration of form can provide opportunities to discover or develop one's unique voice within a context that resonates in the new millennium rather than echoing cultural priorities of the past.

One way to begin this process of trial and error is by ending a reliance on conventions of realism that limit theatrical means and narrative imagination. New forms will surely be inspired by subject matter that arises in the 21st century, for how is it possible to write authentically about the commingling of cultures, technologies, and histories – which is happening all around us – without commingling dramatic forms? Writing in *American Theatre*, in an article titled "Let the Right One In: On Resistance, Hospitality and New Writing for the American Stage" (Jan. 2013), playwright Naomi Wallace articulated the challenge facing playwrights today, a challenge in which the substance of theatre in the new millennium encompasses both form and content.

> In thinking about hospitality, we'll need to consider not only whom we welcome onto the stage but how in our writing we might cross the divide between our own personal experiences and that of others, from our own sexuality to that of another sexuality; our own race to that of another race; our own class and gender to that of another class or gender.
> …
> Sure, our own stories are occasionally interesting, but what I am talking about is connecting our everyday experiences to a worldview, the *longue durée*, the grand narrative, the big picture.

One way to achieve the global perspective that Wallace advocates is by seeking dramaturgical inspiration through an interdisciplinary approach to the subject matter of drama. Since disciplines in the arts, humanities, and natural and social sciences view culture, matter, time, and existence in distinct and different ways, creating a lively dialectic amongst disciplines can generate surprising connections and novel insights, not to mention new possibilities for theatre. With that in mind, I've included in this book four interdisciplinary playwriting projects intended to break with realism by approaching the theatre through other artistic and social forms.

To broaden this discussion of realism/non-realism in the American theatre, I have invited eight accomplished playwrights to share their perspectives on the topic. Each received a series of questions and, as is characteristic of playwrights, they addressed them in various ways. Some answered the questions directly, some took another route, but all of them commented on ways in which their works transcend conventions of realism – and why. I intersperse these remarks with the workshops that follow to introduce fresh vantage points and enhance the creative method developed here through the writing experiences of others.

Also, for this book, three of the most knowledgeable literary artists working with new American plays today – Adrien-Alice Hansel, Tanya Palmer, and Amy Wegener – have identified another eight playwrights. These emerging writers are succeeding in the American theatre – *how?* – by breaking from realism, by attending to a unique voice, concept, or passion that does not fit neatly into a box set. I have no doubt that the tantalizing introductions to these emerging writers and their works will lead you to seek out their plays and track down their productions in future years.

At the core of this volume, is the series of Breaking from Realism workshops I offer to encourage teachers and students to experiment with form. These are open-ended exercises that playwrights at any level of achievement or experience can participate in and benefit from. They are designed to offer an inspirational repertoire of tools, processes, and concepts that can be selectively emphasized, mixed, or matched to effect novel ways of creating and conveying dramatic action.

Along the way, I refer to numerous works, mostly modern and postmodern, to raise awareness of possibilities rather than dig deeply into analysis. Critical thought is essential to creative endeavors, but emphasizing logical investigation and theoretical interpretation can quickly overwhelm an eager imagination and stifle creative impulses. Therefore, the plays cited are intended more as examples for inspiration than as texts for analysis, although they can certainly serve the latter purpose as well. And while this collection of commentary and workshops is conceived primarily for coursework, I hope it may also serve as a provocation for any theatre artist questioning the possibilities and pushing the limits of theatre in the 21st century.

◆ ◆ ◆

All the great successes of the stage are triumphs over convention.

— Emile Zola, *Naturalism on the Stage*

My goal is to provide the next generation of theatre-makers – playwrights especially – with concepts, processes, and tools that will enable them to explore multiple realities on stage and thereby bring to the theatre types of stories and events that are a significant part of the human experience but are not yet a sizeable part of our dramatic repertoire. To accomplish that, we must first acknowledge the characteristics and limitations of realism, the dominant mode of theatrical expression in contemporary American theatre, in order to break from its restraints on artistic expression.

With the notable exception of musicals, which are fundamentally non-realistic, the American theatre of the past century has been dominated by the philosophy and style of realism. In realistic plays time moves forward, characters behave and dress in historically appropriate ways, effects have causes, and action takes place in a familiar world that we can see and touch. Because time, space, causality, and behavior are instantly recognizable, it doesn't take much effort to suspend our disbelief and enter vicariously into the world of the realistic play. As a theatrical philosophy and series of conventions, realism can be extremely effective when used to explore social and political conflicts and to display behavior and feeling. As Anton Chekhov said of his own work, realistic plays attempt to portray "life as it is."

But consider "life as it is" in the 21st century, with its surreal juxtaposition of images and ideas, its complex mix of cultural traditions and beliefs, its unfathomable ability to produce information instantaneously, its revolutionary degree of connectivity, its hyper-awareness of simultaneity, and the myriad ways in which technology mediates life experience. Does realism capture the experience of life in the postmodern era? It does not.

In realistic productions the purposes of scenic artistry are well defined. Lighting is used to evoke time of day or the qualities of its source (fire, lamp, television, etc.). Costumes resemble actual clothing that signifies the socio-economic class, culture, profession, and preference of each character. Sound is the noise or music you'd hear in the place and time of the play. In those design areas, accuracy of detail is as important as atmosphere because, in a realistic play, scenic elements provide vital information about time, place, and character. And so, a second question: does realism exclude opportunities for inventive scenic ideas that might increase the theatrical impact of a production and thereby enliven the audience experience? It does.

The answers to those questions, "no" and "yes" respectively, suggest that future generations of American playwrights should discover or invent new forms of expression that better reflect the experience of life in the 21st century. In his book *Theatre*, scholar Robert Cohen notes, "The theatre has always taken 'real life' as its fundamental subject, so realism seems at first glance to be the perfect style with which to approach the reality of existence." But the content of life and forms of communication in this new century have changed so drastically that surface illusions of realism are unable to contain or convey it. Somewhere along the line we've mistaken "realism" for "reality" and colloquial speech and behavior for "theatricality," and it's time for that to change.

We encounter new subject matter all the time via events, incidents, and stories that people tell, sing, and/or act out. However, we seldom encounter new forms in theatre. Consequently, there's no enlivening artistic dialectic that might encourage playwrights to seek out new and more current forms of expression. Imagine having one story to tell. How quickly would that get old with your friends? The same holds true when there's only one form in which to tell stories on stage.

Creative breakthroughs in any field seldom arrive by chance. They generally require imaginative analysis and an intentional approach that combines critical thought with creative effort. In other words, in their search for new forms of expression, playwrights need to experiment just as scientists do. As with all experiments, some will fail and others will succeed. As Thomas Edison said (and he should know!), "If we knew what we were doing, it wouldn't be an experiment." The attempt is what's valuable, because, when analyzed, failure may be just as instructive as success, if not more so. Furthermore, what seems a failure at first glance might plant the seed of some creative breakthrough years down the line. Only time will tell, but surely nothing innovative will happen if innovation is not consciously pursued.

In 1900, for instance, who could have imagined an angel crashing through a ceiling, an absurd number of empty chairs piling up for invisible guests, or a one-actor documentary exploration of racial tensions that erupted into riots? Even audiences attending premieres of those three plays (*Angels in America: Millennium Approaches, The Chairs, Fires in the Mirror*) were astonished by the novel theatrical forms inspired by changing ethical, social, and aesthetic sensibilities. In the 21st century the pace of change has accelerated. Will the art of theatre keep up with the times? Maybe. Will advances in theatre be led by playwrights as they have been in the past? Maybe. It seems that a break from realistic stage conventions might provide the right opportunity to explore these questions.

Of course, the battle between realistic and non-realistic forms has existed since the writing, staging, and scenic practices of the 19th century coalesced into staging conventions and dramaturgical strategies. There are many reasons for this. Modern technologies and materials allowed designers and artisans to recreate physical environments with convincing precision and detail. Intimate theatres in round or thrust configurations allow actors to speak and behave naturally, since there is no need for an actor's voice or movement to be projected to the back of a distant balcony.

In *The Seagull* Chekhov critiqued both sides of the aesthetic divide with his depictions of the established novelist Boris Trigorin, obsessed with naturalistic detail, and the revolutionary young playwright Konstantin Treplev, who vents his distaste for the trappings of realistic theatre. Reacting against realism and the values of his actress mother, Treplev declares:

> …I don't believe in "theatre," such as it is. She adores the theatre – she thinks she's serving mankind and her sacred art, but if you ask me, our theatre of today is dull and narrow-minded. Every evening, when the curtain goes up, and there under the bright lights, in a room with three walls, those celebrated artists, those high priests of our sacred art, when they play it all out before us, how we mortals eat, and drink, and love, and go around wearing our clothes and leading our lives; when out of this vulgar scenario we are served up some kind of message or moral, however meager, ready for our daily domestic consumption; when after its one thousandth incarnation all these plays seem to me to be the same, time after time the same, then I flee – I flee like Maupassant fled the Eiffel Tower, because it outraged him how enormously trite it was.…
> We need new forms. We must have new forms, and if we don't we might as well have nothing at all.
> [*Translated by Carol Rocamura.*]

Advocates of realism in Chekhov's day saw the theatre as a laboratory in which to observe and consider human behavior with scientific precision. "The essence of realism was *social analysis*," wrote Soviet literary scholar Boris Suchknov in *A History of Realism*. Referring to works by Henrik Ibsen, George Bernard Shaw, and August Strindberg, among others, Suchkov explained:

> The realists were able to portray the essential conflicts of their age which conditioned the inner world of their heroes, their way of thinking and behaving, and to see the sources of social evil that were having such a destructive effect on the human personality.

As realism became the standard mode of theatrical production in the first half of the 20th century, several artistic movements sprang up in reaction to it: surrealism, symbolism, expressionism, absurd-ism, and postmodernism. Whereas the presentation of reality was supposedly "objective" in realism (i.e., the work of the playwright was invisible), the subjectivity of perception, interpretation, and expression were emphasized in non-realistic forms. The popularity of realism has never been seriously challenged in mainstream American theatre (other than by musicals), but the counter-movements have proven influential nonetheless. Over time the conventions of realism have expanded to include inner monologues, flashbacks, and ghosts, all of which are now accepted by audiences as exceptions to the basic tenets of theatrical realism.

A mid-20th century playwright, Tennessee Williams, took up the cause of non-realistic theatre on the American stage. In his "Production Notes" that accompany *The Glass Menagerie*, Williams advocates for a new "plastic" theatre:

> The straight realistic play with its genuine Frigidaire and authentic ice cubes, its characters that speak exactly as its audience speaks, corresponds to the academic landscape and has the same virtue of a photographic likeness. Everyone should know nowadays the unimportance of the photographic in art: that truth, life, or reality is an organic thing which the poetic imagination can represent or suggest, in essence, only through transformation, through changing into other forms than those which were merely present in appearance. These remarks are not meant as comments only on this particular play. They have to do with a conception of a new, plastic theater, which must take the place of the exhausted theater of realistic conventions if the theater is to resume vitality as a part of our culture.

Finally, a playwright in the 21st century, Suzan-Lori Parks, explains (in "Elements of Style," *The America Play and Other Works*) why she transgresses the bounds of realism when writing her plays:

> Form is not merely a docile passive vessel, but an active participant in the sort of play which ultimately inhabits

it. ... We should understand that Realism, like other movements in other art forms, is a specific response to a specific historical climate.

I don't explode the form because I find traditional plays "boring" – I don't really. It's just that those structures never could accommodate the figures which take up residence inside me.... "Repetition and Revision" is a concept integral to the jazz esthetic in which the composer or performer will write or play a musical phrase once and again and again; etc. – with each revisit the phrase is slightly revised. "Rep & Rev," as I call it, is a central element in my work; through its use I'm working to create a dramatic text that departs from the traditional linear narrative style to look and sound more like a musical score.

For several decades now, scenic designers have deconstructed realistic locations in favor of metaphor, atmosphere, and irrationality. Directors and ensembles have devised productions that replace stale stage conventions with striking images, found text, and sensory montage. Artists and composers working in the visual arts, architecture, and music departed from traditional forms long ago. While there are contemporary playwrights who create theatrical worlds with non-realistic elements, American playwrights as a whole are behind the times when it comes to exploration of new forms.

It's important to note that I'm not advocating the exploration of non-realistic expression in the theatre merely for novelty's sake. With the arrival of 100+ channels of 24/7 programming on every electronic device in this era of convergence, stories told through conventions of realism on television and film, as well as in the theatre, seem far more imitative than inventive. Most imaginable variations of stage realism have been explored and exhausted. For audiences, this has resulted in a familiarity with and predictability of form that saps the power of content in artistic expression. Been there. Seen that. Channel surf.

Today, musicals are the only non-realistic theatrical events to surpass realistic drama in popular appeal. There are several clear messages there. In this new millennium of digital entertainment and human interaction mediated by electronic devices, many people look to the theatre less for the illusion of realism than for signs of imagination – for human virtuosity and a more theatrical aesthetic than realism provides.

Again, this problem is not unique to our time. The form, content, and methods of art are fluid and always in flux – or should be, because the continual invention of new forms is needed to speak meaningfully to experience in the present. In his "Preface to *Miss Julie,*" August Strindberg articulated the difficulty of keeping artistically current at the end of the 19th century:

> In other countries people have believed it possible to create a new drama by filling old forms with new contents. For a number of reasons, however, this has failed: … in part because new forms have not been found for the new contents, so that the new wine has burst the old bottles. [*Translated by Harry G. Carlson.*]

For storytellers working in any genre or medium today, this challenge is profound. After decades of immersion in an entertainment and educational culture that privileges realism, young playwrights have internalized the standard modes of thought and expression that those milieux provide. Even beyond television, stage, film, and fiction, the narrative patterns of storytelling that predominate in the United States reinforce the conventions of realism. Lawyers, ministers, advertisers, and politicians use realistic storytelling to make their points. Breaking away from dominant patterns of causality, rationality, and reportage will take concerted effort.

The tools and methods I outline in this book are designed to guide playwrights away from conventions (i.e., limitations) of realism in the pursuit of new forms that are integral to contemporary storytelling. Some challenges that writers may encounter in these explorations of non-realistic forms relate to traditional notions of story on stage and the audience's need for emotion and empathy. However, examples of successful non-realistic plays cited throughout the book clearly demonstrate that formal and theatrical invention can shape story and engage audience empathy by capturing the experience of life as or more profoundly than representational realism.

The premise upon which I've based these workshops, whose goal is theatrical empowerment through formal innovation, is this: When formal elements of art are unfamiliar, it's almost impossible for an artist or writer, working within those forms, *not* to have a creative response. This is true for two reasons: first, there's nothing to imitate so the artist has to innovate; and second, creativity thrives amidst challenge.

The following anecdote demonstrates how struggling with new creative techniques can yield surprising new truths. During an art class, the kindergarten teacher was introducing new techniques of painting to her students, many of whom were having difficulties working with new and strange techniques. While circulating through the classroom, the teacher stopped in front of one student and asked what she was painting. The young girl replied, "God." The teacher looked surprised and explained, "But no one knows what God looks like." To which the girl responded, "They will now."

With such breakthroughs in mind, I have developed Breaking with Realism methods and workshops to encourage originality and, at the same time, thwart the natural tendency to work within a realistic form of dramatic narrative. For young and emerging playwrights, there's a side benefit, as well. Since these exercises don't employ traditional approaches, there's no way to fail because there's no standard against which to measure a writer's effort. It's all an experiment. An exploration. And anything is possible when everything is new.

◆ ◆ ◆

THE SEARCH FOR NEW FORMS: CONCEPTS, PROCESSES, AND TOOLS

It is not true that the stage must remain stationary; it is not true that its actual conventionalities are the fundamental conditions of its existence. Everything marches, I repeat; everything marches forward.

– Emile Zola, *Naturalism on the Stage*

Notions about creativity have changed vastly over millennia. Ancient Greeks believed ideas came from the gods and humans merely implemented divine inspiration. It wasn't until the Enlightenment in the 18th century that humans were credited by philosophers and critics with having creative powers. In fact, it was only 150 years ago that the term *creativity* began to be used in its current sense, which is, according to Webster's dictionary, "the ability to create meaningful new forms and interpretations, i.e., originality."

Today there is a lively discussion amongst educators and artists as to how creativity can be nurtured and developed. Type the word creativity into the search function on Amazon.com, and more than 1,000 book titles appear offering business advice and psychological insights. Two ideas from that avalanche of affirmation inform the design of the Breaking from Realism methodology to follow. First, as Nobel laureate/novelist Mario Vargas Llosa wrote: "You cannot teach creativity – how to become a good writer. But you can help a young writer discover within himself what kind of writer he would like to be." And second, creativity does not play *by* the rules, it plays *with* the rules. That's interesting because creativity in the world of American theatre applies more to *how* things are done rather than *what* is done. The original *what* is rare. The creative *how* is within reach for all of us.

My methodology combines the two aforementioned ideas by making artistic play integral to a writer's quest to become the kind of playwright she or he wishes to be. While it may be true that creativity cannot be taught directly, the underlying premise of the approach in this book is that writers can be taught to play, the result of which is creativity.

The imaginative investigations introduced here all begin with the question "What if?" What if a playwright were able to portray a dizzy universe and not just a dizzy character? What if characters grew or shrank in the course of the play? What if a narrator critiqued the story while narrating it? What if objects spoke, spectacle was theme, character was fragmented, the narrative was incomplete, or dramatic action followed the course of neural pathways?

The Breaking from Realism methodology offers various ways to explore these questions. It presents a series of concepts, processes, and tools that fall outside of the strategies writers would usually or instinctively employ to construct dramatic narratives. I present a series of workshops each offering a novel vantage point. The approach to each is straightforward, the concepts are clearly delineated, and the assignments are open-ended. All of this is designed to reduce the intimidation factor associated with creative work. The methodology takes its cue from Albert O. Hirschman, an economic planner who wrote an essay titled "The Principle of the Hiding Hand":

> Creativity always comes as a surprise to us; therefore we can never count on it and we dare not believe in it until it has happened. In other words, we would not consciously engage upon tasks whose success clearly requires that creativity be forthcoming. Hence, the only way in which we can bring our creative resources fully into play is by misjudging the nature of the task, by presenting it to ourselves as more routine, simple, undemanding of genuine creativity than it will turn out to be.

Finally, in developing the creative methodology presented here I am also inspired by the scientific method: its strategy is one of trial and error through hypothesis and experimentation. Though not a playwright, an advocate of this strategic approach was Thomas Edison, who explained:

> I never did anything worth doing entirely by accident.... Almost none of my inventions were derived in that manner. They were achieved by having trained myself to be analytical and to endure and tolerate hard work.

That's the principle upon which Breaking from Realism is based—only please substitute "hard play" for "hard work."

The Methodology

These descriptions offer a brief overview of the fifteen concepts, processes, and tools that comprise the Breaking from Realism methodology. As you read, you can identify approaches of interest and jump directly to that topic in the Workshop chapter to read a fuller account and exercise plan.

Hybridization

One way to break new ground in any profession is to combine ideas and/or elements from two or more distinctly different disciplines. Often referred to as an interdisciplinary or multi-disciplinary approach, the process of hybridization has yielded centaurs and satyrs, tangelos and broccoli, and dramas like Michael Frayn's *Copenhagen*, which interweaves quantum physics with wartime espionage, Karen Sunde's *Kabuki Macbeth*, whose hybrid sources are self-evident, and Kelly Stuart's *Shadow Language*, which interweaves two journeys: one involves two women on a dangerous picaresque through Turkey while the other uses Karagoz puppetry to delineate events leading up to the deportation and disappearance of a political refugee.

Division and Multiplication

This is about playing with time, space, and identity in ways that an audience can figure out but that the characters cannot see. For example, although scenes may be presented in linear sequence, they are, in the reality of the play, happening in different locations and/or (the audience understands) occurring at the same time. The wizard of this dramatic calculus is Alan Ayckbourn.

His play *Taking Steps* takes place on all levels of a three-story house simultaneously, yet the action is presented on one flat stage with the floors superimposed on each other. The audience is left to figure out this visual puzzle with its strange juxtapositions of characters who may be standing near each other, though they are actually on different floors of the house. It's also possible to divide a character into multiple selves who may appear separately or together on stage. This works effectively in Edward Albee's *Three Tall Women*, Brian Friel's *Dancing at Lughnasa*, and Joan Ackermann's *Off the Map*.

DISTORTION

Messing around with time, scale, and unity can subvert assumptions of realism by calling attention to meanings on the edge of awareness – not through speech and behavior alone, but through distortions of form. Omission, expansion, fragmentation, repetition – any of these techniques can awaken an audience by dislocating their expectations. For example, time passes at different speeds for two brothers in José Rivera's *Cloud Tectonics*. An offstage corpse expands in size in Ionesco's *Amédée, or How To Get Rid of It*. The two characters in David Ives's *Sure Thing* are given countless "do-overs" to overcome social *faux pas* in a valiant effort to connect, which they eventually do. And the fact that Georg Büchner left *Woyzeck* unfinished and with the order of scenes unknown has only increased interest in the play from scholars and directors, who have used the dramaturgical freedom in a variety of inventive ways.

EXPRESSIONISM

Rather than representing the physical world as it appears, expressionist plays present a subjective view that shapes the world by feeling and idea rather than by sight, sound, or touch. Various techniques can be used to accomplish this externalization of thought and emotion: a soliloquy or aside can articulate a thought process, non-verbal behavior can express emotion through action, and a character's viewpoint can be visualized through scenic elements – sound, light, costume, or scenery. In Charles Mee's *Big Love* expressionist moments include distraught women throwing themselves to the ground again and again and men hurling circular saw blades to vent their pent-up fury.

Altered States of Mind and Being

Our lives are colored by many states of mind and physical being, including dreams, dizziness, hunger, rage, exhaustion, paranoia, revelation, lust, confusion, obsession, and panic. When we experience one of those heightened states, our perceptions of the world shift radically. Most playwrights create characters who experience these emotional and/or physical states. However, rather than watch how a character behaves when they are experiencing one of those states, why don't we watch the world take on the qualities of that state? If drama is a mirror held up to life, why not re-focus it to create a world from a state of mind rather than depict a character in action? A mirror can reflect surface images, or it can be used to concentrate light and start a fire.

Bricolage, or Pastiche

Can theatre encompass the unpredictability, chaos, and surreal juxtapositions of life in the 21st century? This is nearly impossible when dramatic events are organized by causality and linear chronology. Bricolage or pastiche, as it is referred to by postmodernists, is constructed by creating a collage from found text, sound, and images which may or may not have any apparent connection. On a moment-to-moment basis, this sequence or simultaneous appearance of disparate elements creates unexpected and often bizarre contrasts, which is the point. With a bricolage play, the observer has more freedom (and responsibility) to make connections and extract personal meaning from the performance. In *Ti Jean Blues,* director/creator JoAnne Akalaitis excerpts, arranges, and incorporates numerous texts by and about Jack Kerouac to evoke that writer's physical and spiritual journeys.

Extreme Symbolism

Who put that rhinoceros on stage? Or all those empty chairs? Eugene Ionesco was a master of extreme symbolism, a technique that transforms a play's essential metaphor into a larger-than-life theatrical image. Another example is Doug Wright's *Quills*, in which the Marquis de Sade's dismembered body parts are brought on stage in boxes in order to squelch his pornographic writing. It doesn't work, and the boxes tremble with pleasure as a hand reaches out from a box and starts to write.

RE-CONTEXTUALIZATION

Whatever actually occurred in the life of Wolfgang Amadeus Mozart, the personality and behavior depicted in Peter Shaffer's *Amadeus* are delightfully twisted in Antonio Salieri's telling of the tale. Salieri's likely exaggerations and misrepresentations are what make the play so engaging, because audiences are left on their own to decipher truths from likely fictions. There's no use pretending that the drama is seen through reliable eyes (i.e., playwright). Rather, letting a character assume the role of a positioned narrator serves to heighten audience awareness of authorial/character intent while adding layers of complexity to the theatrical event. The older Tom provides another example in *The Glass Menagerie*, as does the character Astrakhan in Arthur Kopit's *Becausehecan*.

ANTHROPOMORPHISM

What happens to us as we age? We lose our innocence, yes, but why do we lose touch with so many childhood pleasures? This includes talking objects, animals, and fantasy figures like Spongebob Squarepants, Daffy Duck, Shrek, and Dorothy's trio of non-human pals: Tin Man, Scarecrow, and Cowardly Lion. Such characters are generally relegated to children's theatre, but distinguished playwrights such as Edward Albee and Tony Kushner remind us that talking lizards (*Seascape*) and singing washing machines *(Caroline, or Change)* can illuminate the human condition in unusual ways while providing pleasure to adult audiences. The anthropomorphism of objects, animals, and fantasy figures enlarges the scope of theatrical possibility, expands the realm of metaphor, taps into the collective unconscious of childhood memory, and capitalizes on the element of surprise.

VIRTUOSITY

A great performance can carry a play, so why not write roles that demand something virtuosic from the performer? Whether it's a single talent – operatic singing, circus skills, or quick-change artistry – or some unique combination of skills, virtuosity is part of the heightened experience that theatregoers crave, hence the popularity of Cirque du Soleil. Of course, many kinds of virtuosity are requisite for actors performing plays by Shakespeare or the Marx Brothers, and directors add theatrical wonders like aerial acrobatics to classical plays all the time. The point here is that playwrights can write these performative elements into the action of their plays. *Starlight Express*, for instance, requires in-line skaters to sing, *War Horse* lists a program credit for horse choreography, and playwright A. Rey Pamatmat's play, *Edith Can Shoot Things and Hit Them*, requires an actor to solve a Rubik's Cube in a matter of seconds.

PRIORITY SHIFTS

Aristotle believed in the primacy of plot. Jeffrey Hatcher – playwright screenwriter, and author of *The Art & Craft of Playwriting* – recommends that playwrights focus first on characters, whose motivations and actions create the plot. Both approaches are valid, but so are others. It's possible to conceive of a play in which the dominant factor is environment or music or diction or theme. This concept challenges assumptions of what drives a play. The truth is, any simple definition of a play, such as characters in conflict, proved insufficient long ago to encompass the wealth and variety of dramatic experiences. There's a scene in Adele Shank's adaptation of Virginia Woolf's *To The Lighthouse* in which a shaft of light illuminates objects as it slowly moves across the room; no humans are on stage. A fashion parade featuring dozens of extravagant hats makes its dramatic and political points without any text in Caryl Churchill's *Far Away*. The disembodied mouth in Samuel Beckett's *Not I* makes a terrifying impression as it babbles through a stream-of-consciousness "at the speed of thought."

BORROWED STRUCTURES

Freytag's famous pyramid illustrates the rise and fall of dramatic action as a character confronts obstacles, deals with crises, and reaches a climatic moment before a denouement completes the play. In his explication of Dramatic vs. Epic Theatre, Brecht offers the Epic structure as an alternative to Aristotle's description of plot. One significant difference is that in Epic Theatre each scene stands alone rather than moving via cause and effect through a series of scenes. While Brecht demonstrates the validity of the Epic model with his own plays, his contribution to dramatic theory opens the imagination to other possibilities. Why not structure a play along the lines of a bad night's sleep, a mathematical proof, an interrogation, well, you get the picture. Just as Suzan-Lori Parks is inspired by the repetition and revision pattern of jazz, anything that has an identifiable spatial or temporal structure can provide the template for a dramatic and theatrical experience. In *La Ronde*, for instance, Arthur Schnitzler used the image of a human chain in the shape of a circle to create a series of two-character scenes that trace the circle and end where it began.

THE MYSTICAL, SUPERNATURAL, AND PARANORMAL

Our lives are made more interesting by mystical, supernatural, and paranormal events. Aliens may have replaced fairies in the popular imagination, but wizards and magicians, super-humans and cyborgs, vampires and zombies still rule our fantasies. Psychics and mental telepaths intrigue us to no end. And the twilight zone between ghost and memory plays havoc with our conscience. The public's fascination with other-worldly realms has been fully exploited and generously rewarded by fiction, film, and television. Other than Disney-esque musicals, however, depictions of the eerie and occult are far less common on stage. Why's that? As Naomi Wallace points out in her *Perspective*, "Often the dead are more interesting than the living, and surprising." Other examples include *Tales of the Lost Formicans*, in which Constance Congdon uses aliens to study suburban angst and comment on the disintegration of the American family, and *Bug*, a paranoid drama by Tracy Letts that investigates an *X-Files*-like adventure through madness, fear, and conspiracy theories. The mystical, supernatural, and paranormal are rife with mystery and metaphor that await further exploration on stage.

INTERRUPTION: AUTHENTICITY, CHANCE, CHOICE, AND ACCIDENT

There are many ways to interrupt a play, to draw attention to illusion, to create meta-theatrical moments that enrich an audience's encounter with art. The interjection of someone or something authentic can completely change the terms on which an audience has been participating in the performance. It's one thing to suspend disbelief; it's another to know how to react when the "real" bangs up against the *real*. Luigi Pirandello played with that idea in his "trilogy of theatre in the theatre." Julie Marie Myatt ended her play about the sex trafficking of minors in Cambodia, *Boats on a River*, by replacing adult actresses, who had performed the roles of children throughout the play, with actual five- and seven-year-old girls. The stage convention of adult women playing sexually abused children was blown out of the water by the arrival of *actual* children. Given the subject matter, the impact on the audience was profound. Plays can also employ chance or choice, inviting audience involvement in ways that shape the journey and outcome of a production. Obviously, stopping the action to check in with the audience undercuts any illusion and can strengthen the common bond between actors and audience members. The Neo-Futurists in Chicago, for example, ask audiences to call out numbers corresponding to scenes during their production of *Too Much Light Makes the Baby Go Blind*. Actors then perform scenes in the order that the numbers were shouted, creating random sequences and startling juxtapositions, as well as virtuosic moments, since the goal is to perform 30 plays in 60 minutes. Taking audience participation one step further, actors in the musical *The Mystery of Edwin Drood* ask the audience to select and vote on the ending they'd prefer. (This approach remains true to the novel, which Dickens left unfinished.)

REBELLION

Destruction begets creation. Rebellion is the start of something new. Rejection creates a vacuum, and vacuums have to be filled. Protest is a valid place to look for inspiration – dramatists have often drawn positive energy from acts of negation. The Dadaists, for instance, mocked the insipid rationales for the horrors of WWI with nonsensical performances. In the 1960s, a desire to tear down and replace structures of social conformity and theatrical convention inspired an era of experimentation. Rebellion can not only break through the fourth wall, it can break down the first, second, and third walls, as well. More recently, the Occupy Movement created a powerful theatre of protest on streets around the world in response to the wrongful practices and failed policies of financial organizations.

◆◆◆

...to make theatrical that which is only dramatic...
— Fanny Kemble, *Papers on Acting III*

As playwright Craig Lucas points out in his *Perspective*, "Anything can happen in live theatre, but so seldom does." These workshops are designed to let more things happen. The goal is to challenge playwrights to work in a more conscious way in order to dramatize more of the strange, fantastic, threatening, and surreal aspects of living in the 21st century.

I've conceived these workshops with three assumptions in mind. First, participants bring with them ideas, stories, events, and actions they wish to explore; hence, most workshops begin with a scene or short play that playwrights write or have already written. Second, participants wish to communicate with and affect an audience; thus each workshop involves response and discussion so playwrights can gauge the impact of their theatrical explorations. And third, participants want to experiment and are willing to approach these exercises with an open mind whether or not they buy into the need for and benefits of Breaking from Realism. Healthy skepticism is welcome because it makes creative breakthroughs all the more convincing.

Also, while I don't include multi-media as a specific methodology, I do think that electronic and digital media of the 21st century can be incorporated readily into Breaking from Realism experiments. If playwrights are interested in exploring the potential of mixed media with the goal of better conveying the drama of life in the 21st century, these workshops provide ways to define the purpose and focus the impact of electronic and digital media in live performance.

◆ ◆ ◆

Hybridization

Hybrid forms possess this transformative power, the power to alter, the power to create from what they destroy. When one thing joins with another and becomes something new, the core self is simultaneously retained and annihilated, transformed like the butterfly that completely liquefies inside its chrysalis, reassembling its parts to make a new form.

– Matthew Hittinger,
On the Transformative Power of Hybrid Forms

For an audience, there are two fundamentally different kinds of experience in the theatre. One provides a journey through familiar territory. The other connects topics or ideas that audiences hadn't thought were connected. When well done, both are worthy, but each requires of the writer a different set of creative talents.

The first requires keen observational skills and remarkable insights. A good example is David Lindsay-Abaire's Pulitzer Prize-winning *Rabbit Hole*, which limns the irreparable heartache of a husband and wife who have lost their teenage son in an accident. The subject matter is not unusual, but what sets this work apart from the majority of dramas that explore loss and suffering are Lindsay-Abaire's incredibly detailed characterizations, sharply delineated conflicts, inexpressible emotions, and unconditional compassion for surviving family members who are trying desperately to free themselves from the deadening grip of depression and grief.

The second – connecting the unconnected – relies on a playwright's inventiveness and ability to make a conceptual leap. For example, the combination of Greek chorus and sexual abuse in Paula Vogel's Pulitzer Prize-winning *How I Learned To Drive* makes sense; in fact, the subject matter of injustice, transgression, and guilt seems perfectly suited to the ancient dramatic form. However, linking those elements with teenage driving lessons creates powerful new metaphors that are introduced via situations that are not commonly depicted on stage. In and of themselves, the compelling narrative and cultural taboo are sufficient to make this a powerful drama, but it is Vogel's leap to the driving lesson that gives audiences a fresh perspective on the tragedy of sexual abuse.

This workshop is designed to help writers exploit the creative potential of multi-disciplinary approaches to form and content in dramatic writing. One reason this may not happen more often or on its own is because humans are creatures of habit. Our brains become increasingly hard-wired as we mature, which constrains associative thinking. By the time we reach adulthood, our brains have established neural paths that automatically connect one idea to another. As neuroscientists say, "What wires together, fires together." It takes concerted effort to break mental habits, and one way to derail automatic associations is to purposefully connect the unconnected.

A daily barrage of images, ideas, and events is an inescapable feature of life in the 21st century. Whether you Google, channel-surf , DJ, or multi-task, you can't avoid strange and surreal juxtapositions. In fact, there are professions dedicated to crossing traditional boundaries in order to re-mix ideas, cultures, and materials. Fusion cuisine, eclectic fashion, and postmodern architecture are three, and interdisciplinary approaches in education have led to fields of study such as environmental economics, dentistry engineering, and psychohistory.

The friction of disparate ideas and images on stage creates energy – sometimes as striking as chemiluminescence, sometimes as silly as a jack-a-lope. Playwrights who've tapped this energy include Peter Barnes, whose *Red Noses* combines clowning and foolery with the Black Death in France in 1348, and Steven Dietz, whose surreal monologues in *God's Country* expose the bizarre thought process of white supremacists in ways that the courtroom transcript of the supremacist's actual words can't. The poster-child for hybridization in theatre, however, is *Medea/Macbeth/Cinderella*. Directed and adapted by Bill Rauch and Tracy Young, this volatile concoction interweaves text, characters, and plot elements from the original plays by Euripides, Shakespeare, and Rodgers and Hammerstein. Suffice it to say, it is a wildly entertaining mélange.

THE WORKSHOP: HYBRIDIZATION

The goal of this workshop is to encourage writers to crack open and re-energize basic dramatic conflicts by creating hybrid forms and making strange new bedfellows of incongruous content.

Step 1: **Monologue prompt**. First, before you introduce the workshop, ask writers to chose a very specific subject – beyond the realm of theatre – on which they're quite knowledgeable. This could be related to a job, hobby, book, sport, or any activity or discipline – any arcane morsel of particular information or personal obsession will do. Give them a few minutes to write a brief monologue in which a character grapples with a problem embedded in this subject. The more specifically the character's struggle can be expressed with the terminology and circumstances of the specific subject matter, the better. When completed, put the monologues aside.

Step 2: **Scene prompt**. Again, before you delve into the topic of hybridization, ask playwrights to write a brief scene that has nothing to do with the monologue. The excellent writing prompt that follows is a quick summary of Arthur Kopit's "Did You Bring It?" exercise (featured in *The Playwrights' Workout: Exercises for the Dramatic Imagination from Professional Playwrights*, Smith and Kraus, 2009). Writers will write a brief two-character scene between A and B. The rules: The first line of dialogue in the scene must be "Did you bring it?" Writers must not spend time thinking about the assignment or what "it" is, but rather, should write as quickly as possible – no rewriting allowed. Writers should think of themselves as a fly on the wall overhearing a conversation and writing it down. A and B must be real people having a realistic exchange (no Martians ... for now). Once they discover names for A and B, the writers can use them in conversation, but they must never identify "it" by name.

Step 3: **Introduce hybridization**. Introduce the concept, describe its virtues, and cite examples.

Step 4: **Create a hybrid**. Ask the writers to combine the monologues and scenes that they've written. It shouldn't be as simple as inserting the monologue into the scene. What the writers want is a collision between the two pieces that creates a new form as well as hybrid content. They should work with their original texts as much as possible, but they are welcome to adapt, revise, reshape, and repeat as often as they want.

Step 5: **Read and discuss**. Read the plays aloud. If you have time, read the original scenes, as well. Note what happens to the scenes when this collision of content and form occurs. What strategies did writers use to combine the two pieces? Are the conventions of realism maintained? How unexpected is the combined content, and which work is more interesting – the original scene or the hybridization?

◆ ◆ ◆

PLAYWRIGHT PERSPECTIVE:
Craig Lucas

"Anything can happen in live theater, but so seldom does."

The nature of the stage itself, Theater with a T, invites more possibilities than realism allows. Realism, if done well, is attractive to bourgeoise audiences and critics, because they understand, or think they do, the rules and conventions. They have paid handsomely to feel taken care of. It is the opposite of lived experience, where we are at the mercy of forces we neither apprehend fully nor control. A theater that aims to replicate the experience of being alive as opposed to a contained frame for safely considering aspects of that life – protected from the numinous and terrifying, the unknown, possibly even unknowable, calls for a wider range of tools and artistic options. What does something actually feel like? At first, our instinct is to call upon the known. X is dead as a...The mind helpfully tosses up "doornail" from its vast repository. What this does is protect us from feeling like a child upon first learning about death itself. Wait, do you mean that I myself am going to die? It's impossible! Everyone dies? "Doornail" spares us what the first audience felt hearing the phrase "dead as a doornail" – that gasp of recognition, memory, repetition of maiming emotional trauma. Okay, now we have a tool to DEFEND against ever having to feel that again: "Dead as a doornail." Art that dismantles such defenses is what is required if writers are not to be pandering to people's desires to be distracted, palliated, and serviced.

Lived experience stretches time, skips through years at a glance, goes back, paralyzes, confounds, quickens the pulse, raises a fever, distorts perspective, enrages, and fascinates. One feels other than oneself. One experiences the physical and temporal world beyond the bounds of what we know is real. Anything can happen in live theater, but so seldom does. Oedipus knows the truth but refuses to acknowledge it to himself: What does that experience feel like, the one of knowing but not wanting to know while desperately wanting to know a different answer to the question! Well, it feels like Oedipus. It comes at you from all sides, prolongs the agony and makes the final recognition all-consuming and terrible and fascinating, it requires suicide and blinding and disfigurement and unthinkable courage. That's what makes leaving our homes and behaving properly, sitting quietly and watching in the very same direction as a lot of strangers in a big darkened room without enough leg room and suspending our disbelief sometimes worth the effort. The better that cable TV gets, the less interested anyone is in leaving home to attend theatrical events that resemble cable TV. Musicals, at the very least, offer the chance of replicating one's emotional internal universe.

> *How do you integrate non-realistic theatrical ideas with the conventions of realism?*

Realism requires believable behavior, or one would think that it did if one didn't read mainstream drama critics who like fake, over-the-top phony speech and body-language with British or Irish accents. Anyway, I require believable behavior under extraordinary circumstances to invest in a character's journey, desires, fears. So non-realism depends upon realistic behavior or the illusion of such. If the characters are behaving in extreme, non-realistic ways, I become instantly bored. Even insects behave realistically for insects. Watching people act "larger than life" is a contradiction in terms and it's extremely dull. Like listening to a crazy person, it gets boring really quickly. How one maneuvers through a landscape that feels like a nightmare, now that's interesting. But the behavior is the thing that's interesting, not so much the nightmare. Directors who turn behavior inside out by re-imagining classic plays, making the subtext overt, also bore audiences. We want to see ourselves or people we can understand in situations that feel like the situations we survive daily: full of unimaginable difficulties, confounding dilemmas where no choice is right, surprises, deep disappointments, and always the possibility of redemption through courage or, if nothing else, perseverance.

Does the opportunity to incorporate non-realistic elements in your plays allow you to explore dimensions of the human condition or tell other kinds of stories than the conventions of realism allow?

I believe it does, but I would have no other choice, because my lights tell me that experience, the experience of experiencing, is not realistic. Experience is nightmarish and ephemeral – words don't even fully match the thing itself. Experience is not like the plays of Ibsen. The lack of coherence or safety in the world I inhabit is more like having a 24-hour bug; it spikes with fevers and chills, it tosses me on a sea that feels as if it may quickly consume me. I don't have a choice about what I write, not in the way a realistic play suggests that people have choices. Of course I do have choices, and when I have tried to write realistically or within expected norms or formal requirements inherited from my distinguished forebears, the material grows lifeless quickly. I think for a writer like August Wilson, the conventions of realism served his poetic internal needs, freeing his voices. For me, to be freed to tell things as they are, by which I mean as they feel, I have to work outside of those conventions; otherwise I start to feel that I am working for the Internal Revenue Service at a soul-crushing 9 to 5 job, and if I were going to choose to do that, I would be making more money. So, having tried writing realistic drama, and having waited to try it until I was in my 60s, I now know that it isn't for me. I prefer musicals and plays that aspire to the linguistic and theatrical reach and imaginative possibilities of Shakespeare, Sophocles, Tennessee Williams, Wallace Shawn. Most of what passes as great American drama puts me to sleep, or makes me want to commit crimes.

Craig Lucas *is an award-winning playwright, screenwriter, and director. His plays include* Reckless, Prelude to a Kiss *and* The Dying Gaul, *all of which were subsequently made into films. He wrote the book for the musical* The Light in the Piazza, *the libretto for* Two Boys, *which premiered in 2013 at the Metropolitan Opera, and the book for the musical* King Kong, *which premiered in Melbourne, Australia in 2013. He's received two Obie Awards, the Excellence in Literature Award from the American Academy of Arts and Letters, and both Tony Award and Pulitzer Prize nominations. He received a best screenplay award from the New York Film Critics for* The Secret Lives of Dentists.

◆◆◆

Division and Multiplication

Every morning I jump out of bed and step on a landmine.
The landmine is me. After the explosion, I spend the rest of the
day putting the pieces together.
— Ray Bradbury, *Zen in the Art of Writing*

A playwright's ability to fragment character and/or multiply the number of roles an actor plays provides a dramatic circumstance in which to explore issues of identity and relationship in uniquely theatrical ways. For example, a standard adaptation of *Dr. Jekyll and Mr. Hyde* would utilize both approaches by separating one "person" into two characters and then casting one actor to perform both roles. For the audience, there's double pleasure in this approach – the thematic exploration of a man's divided soul is given bold visual representation through the theatrical magic of an actor's transformative talents.

These two techniques require and reward imaginative participation from an audience. Dividing one character into several qualities or ages presents a level of abstraction that asks audiences to piece together the puzzle of identity. Dramatic fragmentation poses questions about consistency and change in personality over time, internal dissonance, and vagaries of self-knowledge.

According to philosopher Eric Schwitzgebel, our inner lives remain a mystery because we are "poorly equipped with the tools, categories, and skills that might help dissect them." Our internal world, he writes in *Perplexities of Consciousness*, is "gelatinous, disjoined, swift, shy, changeable," and thus belongs to the realm of the irrational. Since realism as a philosophy and form focuses on the observable external features of social interaction, the methods of non-realistic theatre, such as division and multiplication, are essential tools in the exploration of our inner selves.

The most common approach to character fragmentation is when two or more actors represent a single character at different ages. Sometimes this is used to present a character sifting through memories, as with the two Toms in *The Glass Menagerie*, Jean and her younger self, Scout, in the dramatic adaptation of *To Kill a Mockingbird*, and the adult Bo Gordon in Joan Ackermann's *Off the Map*, who looks back on the year when she was eleven and everything changed in her life.

There are also fascinating plays in which characters representing parts of a divided self interact, as they do in Edward Albee's *Three Tall Women*, which portrays a dying woman's search for an understanding of how she became who she is, and Michel Tremblay's *Albertine in Five Times*, which explores how memory can both clarify and confuse recollections across five different decades of a woman's life.

Another thematically imaginative and structurally intricate version of character division is Janet Allard's *Incognito*, in which seven female and seven male actors take turns in the course of a two-character play. Set in the front seats of an automobile, the moments of actor replacement represent change and revelation for two teenagers who are talking through their lives, futures, and relationship.

The flipside to dividing one character into multiple roles is asking one actor to play multiple roles. This choice can provide an actor or actors with a *coup d'theatre,* as it did for Anna Deavere Smith, who wrote and performed more than a dozen roles in her docudrama *Fires in the Mirror*, and Charles Ludlam, whose *The Mystery of Irma Vep* requires numerous quick changes for two actors to create the entire cast of that farcical gothic parody.

The device can also be used to deepen the ties between form and content. In Caryl Churchill's *A Number*, one actor portrays three characters, two of whom are clones of the first. Through this clever investigation of individuality in the age of genetic replication, noted critic Robert Brustein in *The New Republic*, the play suggests that "whatever our genetic inheritance, we are all of us discrete, unknowable individuals."

By using one actor to play identical twins in *Dying City*, playwright Christopher Shinn makes stark the contrast between brothers as they each confront one woman who is central to their troubles. The play takes place in two different years and the time periods are interwoven, causing the actor to exit and quickly re-enter as the other twin, heightening the theatricality of this casting construct. And though Plautus and Shakespeare used this device to create comic confusion, Shinn uses the inevitable contrast between brothers to explore darker truths of distressed souls caught up in love and war.

In Sarah Kane's *4:48 Psychosis*, a character's suicidal thoughts are expressed in the form of "an abstract mindscape," writes critic Mustafa Sakarya in "A Controlled Detonation: The Protean Voice of *4:48 Psychosis*":

> The central 'character' of *4:48* is a writer in the midst of mental and spiritual fragmentation and in many ways, the disjunctive, non-linear structure of the play is a reflection of her fragmentation…

Shortly after writing the play in 1999, Kane committed suicide and left no indications as to how the play should be performed. The Royal Court premiere of the play in 2000 used three actors, and though that was the director's choice, the division of the central voice into three "characters" underscored the process of fragmentation at work on the page and perhaps in the author's mind.

Finally, three actors play twenty characters in *Teechers*, a witty British comedy by John Godber. While having actors play several roles in a play is now common practice in order to reduce cast size and company payroll, Godber uses the device for meta-theatrical purposes. In this play about shortcomings of Great Britain's educational system, three actors/characters put on a play within the play about their experiences with their drama teacher. Each of the three actors/characters performs multiple roles, and they switch off playing their drama teacher, Mr. Nixon. This tri-faceted, cubist approach creates a fascinating portrait by refracting the central character's actions and identity through three minds and interpretations.

WARM-UP EXERCISE

Step 1: **Select.** Each writer selects one of William Shakespeare's plays to be used for both the following exercises.

Step 2: **Divide.** Each writer divides one of the main characters in the plays they've chosen into several roles that make conceptual sense. For example, rather than assign five actors to play Hamlet in each of the five acts, divide up the role by concepts such as crazy or sane, procrastinating or decisive, acting or authentic, calculating or careless. Writers should identify how many actors are needed and where each of them steps in to perform.

Step 3: **Multiply.** Using the same Shakespeare play, writers invent a casting concept and scheme to present the play with five actors or less. Writers need to articulate the thematic/conceptual reason for their scheme and explain which roles each actor will play and why. Remember, in this case the purpose of using a small cast of particular actors is to highlight an interpretation, not to save money. A terrific example is Alan Cumming's one-man performance of *Macbeth* on Broadway in 2013. The play took place in a psychiatric hospital where Cummings played fifteen characters in Shakespeare's bloody tragedy. Cummings was joined by two other actors who portrayed a doctor and nurse.

WORKSHOP: DIVISION AND MULTIPLICATION

This goal of this workshop is to encourage playwrights to theatricalize their works by departing from the realistic equation of one actor/one character.

Step 1: **Write.** Playwrights write a complete scene or, better yet, a short play with at least three characters.

Step 2: **Read and discuss.** Participants in the workshop read the plays aloud so the playwright can listen, then briefly discuss the strengths of each. (They'll want to refer back to the strengths of this first draft later.)

Step 3: **Divide.** Playwrights divide one or more of their characters into several roles by age, quality, attitude, or experience, such as "Hopeful" and "Doubtful", "Dead" and "Alive", "The Road Less Taken" and "The Road More Taken."

Step 4: **Revise.** Writers revise the scene/play incorporating their different versions of the character. Encourage writers to consider how the play's form might be affected by this new construct. Do they need narration, inner monologues, simultaneous action, or time shifts to make sense of the character division?

Step 5: **Read and compare.** What new insights, actions, or theatrical elements have been added to the original script? Has anything been lost in the process of dividing a character into multiple roles? Are the characters more clearly or boldly defined? What kinds of plays might benefit from this approach (memory, schizophrenic, farce)?

Step 6: **Multiply**. Playwrights return to the original scene or short play. This time they will revise their work so that an actor or actors play more than one role. Writers need to identify the thematic or theatrical reasons for their scheme, and they may add characters in order to provide multiple roles for one or more of the actors to play. For example, a three-character play performed by three actors may become either 1) a seven-character play in which two actors play one character each while one actor plays five characters, or 2) a three-character play performed by one or two actors.

Step 7: **Revise**. Playwrights rewrite their play with those new ideas in mind.

Step 8: **Read and compare**. What's been gained and/or lost in this new version? How does increasing acting opportunities affect the theatrical energy or interest of the play? Were the themes or ideas in the play strengthened, complicated, or diminished in this new draft? What kinds of plays might benefit from this approach?

◆◆◆

Distortion

The English language started out as a distortion in my life,
but nothing remains the same, and so the distortion is now just
normal. That is one of the things that will happen to all distor-
tions: They become normal and turn into something else.
                              –Jamaica Kincaid, *Interview on Haaretz.com*

The reason theatre is an art form is because form is indispensible to the art. It defines the overall shape and parts of dramatic action. It refers to the meter and color of dialogue, the arrangement of scenes, the sequence of time, and the frame or frames that contain the action.

The evolution of standard dramatic form is illustrated in a quick history of Western theatre. Aristotle described the formal elements of Greek drama, among them prologue and parados, episode and ode, exodus and epilogue. Horace and the Romans formulated the five-act play, which specified a particular function for each act: exposition, rising action, climax, falling action, and denouement. The neo-classicists insisted on five acts in the Renaissance and, in the 19th century, German playwright Gustav Freytag drew a pyramid to illustrate how the five acts worked together. About that same time, Henrik Ibsen and others experimented with four- and three-act structures, and initiated the 20th century slide into two- and one-act full-length plays.

Currently, mainstream American theatres offer almost exclusively one- and two-act full-length plays; classics with multiple acts are reconfigured into these more compact structures for modern audiences. In recent decades, however, formal deviations have gained notoriety: the multi-part marathon (David Edgar's two-part adaptation of Dickens's *Nicholas Nickleby,* Robert Lepage's three-part epic, *The Dragons' Trilogy*), the now ubiquitous ten-minute play, and the voyeuristic car play in which audience members sitting in the back seat observe theatrical hijinks up front.

Other successful experiments with dramatic form include Caryl Churchill's *Far Away*, a triptych in seven scenes that grows more and more absurd and lasts only 45 minutes, leaving the audience plenty of time for conversation and reflection. Luigi Pirandello contrasted scripted text with "live improvisation" (also scripted) in his meta-drama *Tonight We Improvise*. *Rashomon* presents four versions of one event, leaving the truth unverified at the end. (Fay and Michael Kanin adapted Akira Kurosawa's film, which in turn was adapted from short stories by Ryunosuke Akutagawa – and all were titled *Rashomon*.)

Most playwrights, however, remain satisfied with the standard scene and act structures just as many painters are content to work on a traditional rectangular canvas. For playwrights, that's a missed opportunity, because form offers pleasures of its own alongside the contents that fill it. Playwrights need to investigate formal options that can energize the text and distinguish the narrative – standard form is standard fare.

One way to explore form beyond the norm is to distort the main elements of standard structures, such as time, scale, progression, and completeness. In realistic plays, time moves forward, scale onstage is similar to scale offstage, action adheres to the rules of causality, and a play isn't over unless it's complete. The fun, then, is to find ways to mess around with one or more (or all) of these and still tell a coherent story.

WORKSHOP: DISTORTION

Crack open the weirdness and wonder of contemporary experience by exaggerating or distorting some aspect of our subjective reality – create a world that feels hyper-real, looks surreal, or bends details like a funhouse mirror.

Step 1: **Introduction.** Discuss the four aspects of realism that are ripe for distortion: time, scale, progression, and completeness. Use examples cited above or others to reveal how playwrights in the past have used distortion to empower ideas and embolden theatricality in their plays.

Step 2: **Brainstorm.** As a group, brainstorm ways to mess with each of the four aspects.

Time can stretch or freeze, move backwards or in circles, skip, repeat, or move at different rates for different characters as it does in José Rivera's *Cloud Tectonics.*

Scale can be exaggerated to signify status, diminish importance, or magnify problems, as it does in Eugene Ionesco's *Amédée, or How To Get Rid of It,* in which an offstage corpse in an apartment grows larger and larger and eventually causes mushrooms to sprout. Of course, in stage adaptations of *Alice in Wonderland,* Alice's shrinking and growing requires imaginative design, and once again that's the point – writing can inspire an imaginative rather than illustrative response from a playwright's collaborating artists. (For more on "unstageable stage directions" see Naomi Iizuka's *Perspective.*)

Progression refers to action moving forward according to time and causality, but there are other ways to develop dramatic action. Harold Pinter reverses time and works backwards from effect to cause in his divorce-affair-friendship drama *Betrayal.* Another way to mess with progression is through a repetition of words, scenes, and objects. In *The Chairs,* Ionesco's characters spend their time collecting and arranging dozens of empty chairs for invisible guests until the stage is deluged with chairs and invisible guests. Six or ten empty chairs wouldn't have created an appropriate scenic metaphor for the absurdity of ceremony in our lives. Initially, the repetition of vocabulary on stage has a comic effect, but using and reusing a single word or phrase can push meaning itself into the realm of the absurd by demonstrating the limitations of meaning and even the tyranny of language. And in *Sure Thing,* David Ives gives two characters many chances to erase their social *faux pas* in the course of an awkward encounter by backing up and trying again ... and again ... and again, until they manage to connect.

Completeness explains the dramaturgical urge to tie up loose ends, pay off sub-plots, nail down metaphors, and answer or at least clarify questions that arise in the course of the play – providing, of course, a climax and denouement. On the other hand, "incomplete" implies unfinished even though a play's parts are often as or more interesting than the whole. One of the oft performed classics of the past century is *Woyzeck*, which was left in a fragmentary state when its author, Georg Büchner, died at the age of 23 in 1837. The fact that the play was unfinished – even the order of scenes is debatable – has served less as obstacle to future production than as an invitation. The 19th century text has been adapted into musicals, films, puppet theatre, opera, and ballet, and several stage productions have highlighted the uncertainty of scene sequence by scrambling the order of scenes for each performance. Edward Albee's *Fragments* creates a theatrical journey with a series of stories that provide, appropriately, only snippets of the characters' lives. That's similar to the stage adaptation of Edgar Lee Masters' *Spoon River Anthology*, which consists entirely of concise, highly selective, self-reflective commentaries. In both cases, the authors create an unsettling composite of human experience through a process of accumulation, both narrative and thematic, rather than focusing on conflict leading to climax and denouement.

Step 3: **Write.** Begin with short plays that participants bring to the workshop or scenes they write before delving into the discussion of distortion. The goal of the exercise is for writers to distort form in order to exaggerate or intensify a thematic point or dramatic conflict. Writers should focus on one element at a time (scale, time, progression, completeness), so the entire workshop requires four separate drafts of the original scene or short play.

If participants write scenes at the beginning of the workshop, an excellent prompt is Arthur Kopit's *Did You*

Bring It? exercise. (A full description of the exercise is featured in *The Playwright's Workout*, published by Smith and Kraus.) The basic details are these. Writers begin a scene with the phrase "Did you bring it?" They should not know anything else about the scene except that it consists of two characters and "it" should never be identified by name, though the audience may understand what "it" is. Writers should not prepare, everything they need to know will be discovered in the act of writing, such as location, characters' names, and the need for "it". No re-writing allowed, and scenes about drugs and prophylactics should be avoided because the topics are familiar and predictable.

Step 4: **Read and discuss**. Read the scenes aloud and discuss how distortion affects content and audience engagement. Has distorting time, scale, progression, or completeness made the play more intriguing, surprising, mysterious, funny? Has the main idea of the scene shifted? Is the work more theatrical, in what ways?

◆◆◆

PLAYWRIGHT PERSPECTIVE:
Melanie Marnich

"When time warps or bends in my plays... it's because I feel that in real life, at certain times, it feels like time speeds up, slows down, plays in loops..."

I never think that I'm writing non-realistic elements. I think that I'm writing realism – or at least finding ways to convey emotional realism. The scenes and theatricality I try to create simply feel true to me. Authentic and relatable. A conventional "he says...then she says...then he says..." followed by an efficient transition between scenes... then back to "he says and she says..." that's what feels unrealistic to me. I enjoy it, but it often looks and sounds foreign to me. A language I don't really understand on a stage.

I like to think of my style as something I call "hysterical realism" – the physical/theatrical manifestation of rich/heightened/confusing or overwhelming emotions that we feel every day as part of our reality. I don't know about other people, but I think life is weird and surprising and absurd (and often funny). The theatrical elements in my plays are honestly my ways of capturing how life feels to me. The inspiration for these moments comes from regular old life – the key and crucial moments, of course. It would never dawn on me that I have to figure out how to integrate them with conventions of realism. Like I said, I think I am writing realism – I'm just making what we feel internally...external.

When time warps or bends in my plays... it's because I feel that in real life, at certain times, it feels like time speeds up, slows down, plays in loops...fucks with your head and your heart and your intellect. And yes, it does let me explore "dimensions of the human condition" – in a way that can only be created on stage. That's very important to me when I write a play.

The fact is, when I'm writing, I sit back, close my eyes, and ask myself: What does this emotion look like and what does it do to this character's perception of the world around her. When I see this – I start to see the play...

MELANIE MARNICH *is an award-winning playwright and television writer. Her plays include* Quake, These Shining Lives, Tallgrass Gothic, Blur *(Francesca Primus Prize),* A Sleeping Country *(Mickey Kaplan New American Play Prize), and* Cradle of Man *(Carbonell Award for Best New Work of the Year). Theatres that have produced her work include New York's Public Theater, the Royal Court Theatre, Guthrie Theater, Manhattan Theatre Club, Arena Stage, the Actors Studio, Actors Theatre of Louisville, and Commonweal Theatre Company. As a staff writer for the HBO drama* Big Love, *Marnich was nominated for the Writers Guild of America Award for episodic drama. She currently writes for the Showtime series* The Big C.

◆ ◆ ◆

Expressionism

Reality is wrong. Dreams are for real.
— Tupac Shakur, *www.tupacquotes.org*

Expressionism is a well-known genre of art and literature that externalizes and makes manifest in action, setting, and symbol the subjective aspects of human experience. Here are two examples from Charles L. Mee's *Big Love*, which updates what some believe is the oldest surviving drama in the Western world, *The Supplicant Women* by Aeschylus. In this serio-comic commentary on sexual politics, Mee externalizes the inner angst of his characters with bold theatrical gestures. The first tirade accentuates the angry feelings of Thyona, an unwilling bride-to-be, with violent physical actions.

THYONA: ...You think you can do whatever you want with
    me, think again.
    you think that I'm so delicate?
    you think you have to care for me?
    You throw me to the ground
    you think I break?
       [She throws herself to the ground.]
    you think I can't get up again?
    you think I can't get up again?
       [She gets up.]
    you think I need a man to save my life?
       [She throws herself to the ground again.]
    I don't need a man!
    I don't need a man!
       [She gets up and throws herself to the ground again and
       again as she yells.]
    In this next speech, Oed (pronounced Ed, but spelled Oed as in Oedipus) extols the virtues of male bonding in a Robert Bly-inspired tribute complete with circular saw blades. Note how the choice of props (power tools) underscores the manliness of Oed's argument.

OED: ... these men,
    they understand
    because this is **what it is to be a man**
    men know about this
    because **they have gone through it**
    and **they remember**
    they know the pain,
    they don't want to talk about it
    they try to hide it
    but if you open up to them
    they'll open up right back

> *[Oed rips off his shirt and throws it to the floor, picks up circular saw blades, one after another, from a pile of saw blades, and hurls them across the stage so they stick in the side of another building that has been wheeled into place, yelling, for no good reason other than that he has gotten himself worked up...]*

Eugene O'Neill uses another expressionistic technique in his 1928 Pulitzer Prize-winning play, *Strange Interlude*, which was hailed at the time by critic George Jean Nathan as: "The finest, the profoundest drama of his entire career." The *Boston Transcript* critic noted that the play affirmed O'Neill's "ambition to widen and deepen the scope of the stage," which is exactly what we're after with these workshops.

It's worth noting that those reviewers were moved just as much by the novelty of the play's non-realistic form as they were by the more conventional revelation of the play's central character. What was highly unusual about the drama was this: O'Neill revealed his characters' inner thoughts and feelings directly to the audience via "asides" before those thoughts and feelings were expressed in dialogue to other characters on stage. This expressionistic device made the audience insiders to the characters' motivations and intentions. Throughout the six-hour performance, the audience followed two separate worlds: an outer objective reality and inner self-conscious reflections. The result was, according to Brooks Atkinson of the *New York Times*, "a psychological novel of tremendous power and depth put into the theatre instead of between the covers of a book."

WORKSHOP: EXPRESSIONISM

Strong passions animate characters, which empowers dramatic action and focuses audience interest. The goal of this workshop is to encourage playwrights to amp up the theatricality of a scene or play by imagining how characters might express themselves in ways other than naturalistic behaviors and realistic conversation.

Step 1: **"Locked Room".** In a location they cannot escape (it doesn't need to be a locked room, it could be a boat or a ski lift, for instance), two characters engage in a contest of wills. Character A wants something badly but Character B stands in the way. Character B may also want something that A refuses to relinquish. Using this basic scenario, each playwright writes a scene in which the characters employ several strategies to get what they want – until at least one of them does…or both don't.

Step 2: **Identify Subtext.** Ask writers to find several moments in the scene where the dialogue doesn't fully or adequately express the thoughts or feelings of the characters.

Step 3: **Externalize.** First, writers use O'Neill's idea of "asides", so that characters step out of the scene for a moment and share their feelings or thoughts directly with the audience. Afterwards, they step back into the scene and continue the action. The playwrights write these moments into their Locked Room scenes. Second, ask writers to imagine an exaggerated behavior or action that expresses the full force of an unexpressed emotion, desire, or need of a character. The playwrights now write that behavior or action as a stage direction and add it to their Locked Room scenes.

Step 4: **Read and Discuss.** Read the scenes aloud – both versions, before and after expressionist revisions. Discuss the differences between the scenes. Which was more interesting? What was gained in theatrical energy or character revelation? Was anything diminished or lost? Did the expressionistic moments enhance or detract from the overall dramatic interest or pace of the scene?

◆ ◆ ◆

Altered States of Mind and Being

There is no interest in achieving the possible, but it is exceedingly interesting to perform the impossible.
– Serge Diaghilev, *Serge Diaghilev and the Ballet Russes, 1909-1929: When Art Danced with Music*

Realistic plays present the outward appearance and recognizable psychology of characters in a material world that follows accepted laws of physics. But material consciousness – our awareness of things in motion and at rest – is not the only way we experience our lives. Sometimes we're dizzy and the world spins, or our memory fails us and things aren't where or what we remember them to be, or we dream of events that break the laws of physics. These are examples of altered states of mind and being. Others include dementia, changes to the brain through injury or stroke, substance use and abuse, confusion, spiritual transcendence, hallucination, supernatural encounters, and paranoia, to name a few. A neurologist, Oliver Sacks, discusses more exotic examples in his books, *An Anthropologist on Mars* and *The Man Who Mistook His Wife for a Hat: And Other Clinical Tales.*

Characters suffering various disorienting conditions have appeared in plays and on stage. What is seldom presented, however, is a depiction of how the world appears from the point of view of the person experiencing the disorientation. What does a dizzy world look, sound, and feel like? What's it like to live in a world where memory and reality don't match? Or a world where you don't know anyone, though they seem to know you? Or a world that's blurry, confused, caffeinated, or doesn't obey the laws of physics? Or a world in which a hat claims to be your wife?

Can these profound life experiences be explored in the theatre? Arthur Kopit accomplishes this in *Wings,* which depicts the world as it might appear to a stroke victim – a collage of fragmented thoughts, voices, and images. A theatrical universe that operates on the laws and logic of heightened emotions, otherworldly encounters, or rare neurological conditions can lead a playwright on an enlightening journey into what it means to be human.

Workshop: Altered States of Mind and Being

This workshop asks playwrights to evoke a state of mind or being on stage by coloring a theatrical universe with characteristics a person might associate with that state mind or being. These plays offer a different kind of experience for audiences who are used to plots that are structured along the lines of Freytag's pyramid – unusual perhaps, but no less valid or interesting.

Step 1: **Brainstorm**. Ask writers to think of examples of altered states of mind and being and list them on a board or giant Post-it, if possible. Divide the writers into small working groups. Each group selects one altered state and brainstorms a list of characteristics associated with that mental condition. For example, dizziness would be characterized by a world that's wobbly, causes nausea, spins, falls down, etc.

Step 2: **Create that world.** Ask each working group to collaborate on writing a single dramatic scenario that takes place in the world of the altered state. For example, a man wants to go for a drive, but his wife – the Hat – won't give him the keys.

Step 3: **Write that scene.** Each playwright now writes his or her version of the scene that the group created, using as many characteristics of the altered states as possible to define the world, not the character. Playwrights will probably use lots of stage descriptions and directions – and that's all right. They're re-imagining the possibilities of theatre, and that's the point.

Step 4: **Read and discuss.** Playwrights read their scenes aloud. Discuss how the world of the play embodies or conveys the state of mind. Did the play feel, look, and/or sound like the altered state? Did the world obey the unique laws and logic of the altered state, or did the scene simply offer a portrait of a character caught up in the altered state (dizzy world or dizzy character)? What's the likely audience experience of these scenes or short plays – will they sense the altered state though it's not explicitly stated? Ask the students to imagine staging some of their scenes without many resources and on a small budget? Can imaginative and inexpensive solutions be as or more interesting than multi-million dollar stage or film creations?

◆◆◆

Altered States Of Mind And Being – A Play

Written by Bevly Anderson during a workshop at the Inkwell Theatre in Washington, DC, this play imagines a universe formed from the symptoms of someone who's been drugged with Sodium Pentathol – the truth serum. The characteristics of that state of mind include grogginess, relaxation, hallucinations, garbled speech, babbling, exaggerated or intensified emotions (guilt, sadness, lust, etc.), and exaggerated reflexes. The twilight consciousness brought about by the injection of Sodium Pentathol lasts at most 5-10 minutes.

And the Truth Serum Will Set You Free
    by Bevly Anderson

Cast:
    Subject
    Top Chef #1
    Top Chef #2
    Door

> *(Complete darkness. A babbling brook is heard. Dim lights up on the Subject, seated in a chair, facing audience, hands on the armrests, chin down. He's in a small room with one door. Behind and suspended above him, a large analog clock. We see its hands stop. Subject struggles to lift his head and look around. Slowly, over the background sounds, voices emerge. Top Chef #1 and Top Chef #2 are dressed in lab coats. Their voices are distorted, loud and echoing. As the Chefs enter, the Door walks away from the door frame to let them pass.)*

TOP CHEF #1: Hello. My name is Dr. Gordon Ramsay…
TOP CHEF #2: …and I'm Dr. Paula Deem! What's YOUR name?

(Subject says nothing. Through the open door frame we see images projected in the room beyond. These are images/hallucinations that pass through the Subject's mind, flashing colors, family photos, product advertisements, food, sex.)

CHEF #1: What did he say? WHAT DID YOU SAY?

CHEF #2: What's YOUR name? WE'RE HERE TO HELP YOU!

(Subject says nothing. Images flash.)

CHEF #1: Would you like some water?

(Sound of babbling brook gets louder.)

CHEF #1: (*To Subject.*) It's no good resisting...

CHEF #2: Would you like something to eat?

(Suddenly the lights pop to bright on Subject as his head comes up and his eyes open wide. The hands on the clock reverse direction and will, through the following, pick up speed, spinning ever faster. From side of the chair, the Subject pulls out a chef's hat and puts it on, from under the chair, he pulls out a bowl, and from various places on the chair or even within the chair he liberates a large knife, several ripe peeled avocados, two halves of a lemon, a large salt cellar, a wooden spoon, peeled tomatoes, and – for good measure – an egg or two, and an onion. A table mysteriously slides in front of him. He plonks all the ingredients on the table. With intense and furious energy, he begins to hack away at the onion, flinging pieces into the bowl. He begins to cry. The Door moves closer to watch this.)

SUBJECT: I can't remember the recipe!

CHEF#2: Ahhh,...but that's not really the problem. You really should help us. We're nice people...

CHEF#1: ...very nice!

SUBJECT: That's true.

CHEF#2: And not to help nice people...well...that would be...

CHEF#1: ....ah...ungrateful?

CHEF #2: YES! Ungrateful! And I don't sense that YOU'RE like that at all! You're not, are you? Ungrateful?

SUBJECT: *(sobs)* No.

CHEF#2: So…we need to know how much uranium….

(Subject flings the remainder of the onion into the bowl. He proceeds to squeeze the tomatoes into the bowl with great intensity and evident pleasure, wiping the remains all over his face. The door sits down in the Subject's chair. The lights fade slowly. It gets dimmer and dimmer.)

SUBJECT: Two…toe-toe-toe….

CHEF#1: Two…tons? *(To Chef #1)* Jeez! That can't be right…

CHEF#2: *(To Subject.)* Tons? Two tons?

(Subject finishes with the tomatoes, a bloody mess, and proceeds to mash the avocados together between his hands. Some of it actually goes into the bowl. The Door leans back and lights up a cigarette.)

SUBJECT: Two…avo..cah…cah…cah…ummmmmmmm.

CHEF#1: We're running out of time here.

CHEF#2: Where is the uranium coming from? Where was it shipped from?

SUBJECT: *(Ecstatic)* Gua…

CHEF#1: Gua…ta…?

SUBJECT: Mmmmo-lay.

(Subject, having dispensed with the avocados, is sucking his fingers and spitting avocado remnants into the bowl. With each lick of the fingers, the lights flicker. The Door gets the "whips"; will it fall asleep?)

CHEF#1: Guatemala?

CHEF#2: Don't put words in his mouth!

CHEF#1: I'm not putting anything in his mouth. Thank you!

(The lights brighten again, and at once, Subject becomes more hyperactive – squeezing the lemons

into the bowl with obvious pleasure. He cracks the eggs on his forehead and tosses them into the bowl. Big dollups of salt from the salt cellar. He picks up the wooden spoon and begins to frenetically stir the contents of the bowl. The Door is startled awake, looks around, stands up and watches.)

CHEF#1: Look here! You…yes, you! *(Slapping the Subject lightly, back and forth across his face and spreading more avocado and tomato and egg pieces about.)* We need to know where the uranium was SHIPPED FROM…

SUBJECT: Mexico…originally, of course.

CHEF#1: Have you got that?

CHEF#2: Two tons of of guacamole to Mexico?

CHEF#1: Where is NOW? C'MON, WHERE IS IT NOW?

(Subject stares at Chef #1 and Chef #2 quizzically, sucking on the wooden spoon. The Door shakes its head and moves back to the door frame. Images still flashing on the back wall.)

SUBJECT: Holland….?

CHEF #1 and CHEF#2: Holland!

SUBJECT: – daise. *(Pause.)* Sauce.

(Chef #1 and Chef #2 look at one another and sigh. They taste the guacamole.)

CHEF#2: Not bad.

CHEF#1: Right. Shall we go for dessert?

(Chef #1 pulls out a hypodermic syringe and prepares to inject the Subject with a different substance. The Door steps into the door frame, fits perfectly. Swings closed. Lights begin to fade, the clock hands begin to move slowly in the appropriate direction and all sounds fade. With the injection comes darkness and silence.)

THE END

◆ ◆ ◆

Playwright Perspective:
Lee Blessing

"...much of the movement to non-realistic styles springs from the perception that we playwrights are serving an ever-more sophisticated audience..."

I suppose I've always thought of myself as living in a world reflected in both realistic and non-realistic ways by the dramatic art around us. Some of my earliest influences were Theatre of the Absurd authors: Beckett, Genet, Ionesco, Pinter to a degree and even Albee. I couldn't really write like them at the time (met with unqualified disaster whenever I tried), but even as I turned back more and more to realism, I never abandoned my admiration for the worlds they created. My early plays were realistic endeavors, but beginning with the heavy use of direct address in *Eleemosynary*, I found more and more opportunities to introduce non-real elements into some of my works.

My play *Two Rooms*, primarily a realistic play, makes use of non-realistic scenes between a kidnap victim in Beirut in the 1980s and his wife back in Washington, D.C. These scenes are presented intermittently with realistic scenes, and no unusual effects are employed to "separate" them from the rest of the play or signal the audience that an "impossible" scene is taking place. The play simply alternates real and non-real scenes fluidly, relying on the audience to understand and accept the right of each style to exist in the play and the overall usefulness of seeing them work in concert.

Similarly, *Down the Road* employs a strategy of moving more and more as the piece progresses from a strictly realistic style to one that's clearly non-real by the end. A serial killer whom we see early in the play being interviewed in prison has, by play's end, "invaded" the motel room where his interviewers are staying. The interviews continue, but in a meta-world with elements of both locations. At one point, he's even seen in bed with one of his interviewers.

Plays like these are certainly at base realistic works. But I used non-real elements to allow them to "stay ahead" of the audience and to make some thematic points all the more powerfully, if possible. I generally think much of the movement to non-realistic styles springs from the perception that we playwrights are serving an ever-more sophisticated audience, which (since the Absurdists, at least) has less and less difficulty making the leaps that non-realistic styles demand. Also, this audience (as is always the case, I suppose) is looking for something new, something which will fire their imagination and keep their minds open to new and challenging ideas and perceptions. In a way, non-realistic styles are simply a new "toy" for audiences of our era to be distracted by, while we playwrights continue our eternal task of slipping the thematic knife between their aesthetic ribs, so to speak. Plays always have to mislead, misdirect, and distract in order to "land" ultimately – in order to hit home. Non-realistic elements are one more tool for accomplishing that job.

Since 2000, I've employed non-realistic elements in my plays to a greater degree – so much so that in some plays, like *Black Sheep* and *A Body of Water*, it might be argued that for the first time in my work the realist elements are ultimately more in service to the non-realistic ones than vice-versa. These plays feel more mystical to me, more subject to individual interpretation rather than being works that try to forge a narrow, particular, unified point of view in their spectators. I like the thought that those who see *A Body of Water* may be forced to entertain the thought that nothing they know is provable in an absolute sense. In writing *Black Sheep*, I "assigned" myself the task of making one impossible thing occur in each of the play's otherwise realistic scenes, simply to see how that would affect our perception of this world of the very rich, thus underscoring the point that for the very rich nothing is truly impossible, and that their lives – to the rest of us at least – truly appear to exist as if by magic.

A more recent play, *A User's Guide To Hell, Featuring Bernard Madoff*, takes place literally in Hell. While it has a clear and logical narrative, its setting is by definition non-real and absurd. But putting Bernie Madoff anywhere else simply felt beside the point. Even though he's Jewish and presumably doesn't believe in Hell, the fury of our general condemnation of him actually requires a Hell, thus it easily becomes "real" for us as a backdrop while we examine who he is, what he's done, what he deserves, and what responsibilities we ourselves must own for his very existence.

Another play with a non-real setting is *When We Go Upon the Sea*, which takes place in The Hague, the night before George W. Bush is to be tried in the World Court for his crimes while President of the United States. Obviously this had not happened by the time I wrote the play in 2007, and of course it has yet to occur. It's absurd of course, because it can't occur. As a legal matter, the United States is not subject to this court and probably never will be. Still, our presumed "need" to see justice done and responsibility taken for the dismal international record of his war-mongering administration makes an audience willing to spend this fictional "night" with the play.

LEE BLESSING'S *plays have been produced on Broadway (*A Walk In the Woods*) and off Broadway (*A Body of Water, Going to St. Ives, Thief River, Cobb, Chesapeake, Eleemosynary, and* Down the Road*), at theatres across the U.S. (Manhattan Theatre Club, La Jolla Playhouse, Yale Repertory, and Actors Theatre of Louisville), as well as internationally in Japan, South Africa, France, Brazil, Russia, and London's West End. The Signature Theatre in NYC dedicated a season to Blessing's work in 1992-93. Blessing has received The American Theatre Critics Circle Award, The L.A. Drama Critics Award, and The Great American Play Award, as well as Tony Award and Pulitzer Prize nominations.*

◆ ◆ ◆

Anthropomorphism

Four legs gooood, two legs baaad!
> — George Orwell, *Animal Farm*

Anthropomorphism is the act of ascribing human attributes to non-human fauna, flora, ideas, and material objects. Many nursery rhymes, allegories, and fables use this technique: the cup runs away with the spoon, Brer Rabbit fools Brer Fox, the tortoise beats the hare. For older children, there's *The Wizard of Oz*, featuring Dorothy's three singing-and-dancing non-human friends. And for adults, there's Audrey, the man-eating plant in *The Little Shop of Horrors*: "Feed me, Seymour!"

The animation and humanization of objects has been used for poetic and political effect in more serious works by Federico García Lorca and Tony Kushner. In Lorca's *Blood Wedding*, the Moon serves as a Greek chorus, commenting on the action and then denying the lovers the darkness required to escape their pursuers, who find and kill them.

MOON:…

> I want no shadows. My rays
> must get in everywhere,
> even among the dark trunks I want
> the whisper of gleaming lights,
> so that this night there will be
> sweet blood for my cheeks,
> and for the reeds that cluster
> at the wide feet of the wind.
> Who is hiding? Out, I say!
> No! They will not get away!
> I will light up the horse
> with a fever bright as diamonds.

> *[Translated by James Graham-Luján and Richard L. O'Connell]*

In the musical *Caroline, or Change*, Kushner wrote lyrics for a washing machine, clothes dryer, and radio to articulate the titular character's internal debate over what to do with a quarter she finds while washing her employer's laundry.

THE WASHING MACHINE: Little reward.
CAROLINE: Shouldn't take it.
THE WASHING MACHINE: Little present.
CAROLINE: I don't need it.
    …
THE WASHING MACHINE: Little money to be spent
little bit of supplement.
CAROLINE: Can't afford the embarrassment.
THE WASHING MACHINE AND RADIO: Take it home.
CAROLINE: Money don't buy happiness.
THE WASHING MACHINE: Pocket change for…
THE WASHING MACHINE AND RADIO: Sayin' Yes!

When objects are anthropomorphized in the theatre, familiar themes like forbidden love, social justice, and racial politics get a fresh look because we rarely, if ever, hear from objects, and their perspectives are often unique. Also, because inanimate objects bring symbolism to the stage, an audience has more content to interpret, which generally makes plays more interesting.

There's a scene in the film *Tootsie* where Dustin Hoffman's character, Michael Dorsey, defends his portrayal of a tomato in a commercial. His agent, George, played by the director/producer of the film, Sydney Pollack, accuses Michael of alienating everyone in the entertainment industry by arguing about everything, which wastes time and money. George points out that, during the filming of the commercial, Michael wouldn't sit down as directed. This exchange follows:

MICHAEL: It wasn't logical.
GEORGE: You were a tomato! A tomato doesn't have logic!
    A tomato can't move!
MICHAEL: That's what I said. So if he can't move, how's
    he gonna sit down, George? I was a stand-up tomato, a

juicy, sexy, beefsteak tomato. Nobody does vegetables like me. I did an evening of vegetables off-Broadway. I did the best tomato, the best cucumber. I did an endive salad that knocked the critics on their ass!

There are no rules or boundaries in anthropomorphism, and Michael doesn't seem too concerned that he undercuts his own argument when he points out that he was a "stand-up tomato." Stand-up or sitting down, Michael's adamancy draws our attention to the power of anthropomorphized characters. Dustin Hoffman/Michael does a great job creating and then portraying a female actor named Tootsie, but the film still leaves me wanting to see Michael's performance as a tomato.

WORKSHOP: ANTHROPOMORPHISM

This workshop asks playwrights to imbue objects, animals, or plants with human consciousness and the ability to join in the games we humans play. In other words, "Rose is a rose is a rose is a rose" ... that can talk.

Step 1: **Object Theatre Festival.** Playwrights will write and "perform" a play in which the characters are objects which the writers bring to the workshop. Object theatre is similar to puppet theatre – the writers manipulate and speak for the objects that move like objects might – but the objects remain objects and don't become human. (Think Mrs. Potts and Chip, the tea kettle and tea cup, in *Beauty and the Beast*.)

Step 2: **Research.** Watch You Tube videos of commercials and animated sketches in which the characters are anthropomorphized objects, plants, or animals. Discuss which characteristics are human and which belong to the object? Are the object's wants and desires consistent with the properties of the object? How well do human emotions fit the actions of the object?

Step 3: **Pre-Writing.** Playwrights bring two or more objects to class. They list ten basic characteristics of the objects (e.g., a ball is round and rolls, a paper lays flat and its edges cut, a spoon can dish out honey or poison). Second, writers consider what human traits the objects may have. Speech and movement are the main ways humans express themselves. How does the object move? Does it hop, bounce, roll, topple – or is it stuck in one place? Is it young or old? Does it come from a region of the world where people speak a language other than English or a dialect? Third, writers consider what problems the objects may have. Pens run out of ink and are disposable. Apples get old and wrinkled. Tomatoes are often squashed before being cooked. Finally, writers identify a dramatic action and conflict that arise from "life problems" distinctive to the object.

Step 4: **Write.** An object play benefits from the fundamental elements of dramatic writing: action, character development, conflict, and climax. Object plays are also relatively short, usually two to three minutes in performance.

Step 5: **The Festival.** Each writer performs his or her object play alone or with the help of others. The writers speak for and move the objects according to their properties. As always, rehearsal helps ensure a lively and confident performance.

Step 6: **Discussion.** A great object play walks a line between human and object worlds, using elements of each along the way. Some plays become allegories or parables, while others reveal surprising similarities between objects and people.

Step 7: **Video.** It can be useful and enjoyable to video-record performances and replay them so that writers can view their work. Focus the camera on the objects rather than the object manipulators.

◆◆◆

ANTHROPOMORPHISM – A PLAY

The following play, *Full Measures* by Tony Del Grosso, was written in an undergraduate playwriting course at Transylvania University. The anthropomorphized Piano, Staccato, and Marcato illustrate how characters can be inspired by concepts as well as objects.

Four Measures
by Tony Del Grosso

> *Lights up on a piano in the center of the stage. A bench is set in front of the keys. The piano looks to be an extremely old model and the keys are yellowed with age. A key or two are missing and some are out of tune. Stage is set up like a concert hall, with chairs arranged in staggered formation for audience, all facing the piano. A MAN in full tux attire walks on stage. He walks to the front of the piano, turns to the audience, bows, and sits on the bench. He has with him a book of music and begins to play. Instead of music being produced from the sounds, a slow babbling of voices grows from the piano, overlapping each other and creating a piece out of the words themselves. An older WOMAN climbs out of the piano, followed by two others, MARCATO and STACCATO. The WOMAN speaks, her voice is melodic, almost a song, but has a tendency to go flat mid-sentence.*

WOMAN: Who is there?

> *The voices subside and she is left staring at the man playing the piano. The piano makes no noise at this point. It is as if the WOMAN is being sustained by the notes. The WOMAN speaks to the others, who each have their own melodic genre of speech.*

WOMAN: The last time was in a dusty storage room.

STACCATO: The time before that. It was in the garage. Of some middle-class homeowner. Fingers like clubs. Dexterity of a walrus.

MARCATO: **The time before that was in an elementary school auditorium, the one least used, covered by a sheet until the annual children's concert.**

STACCATO: The time before that. Rockefeller Center. The Radio City Music Hall.

MARCATO: **The time before that was at Cherkassky's fingertips.**

WOMAN: And the time before that was in a factory as a scale architect plucked and tuned my body until I was pristine.

(Pause)

Next time, it will be the parting notes of scissors cutting through my strings, wrenches removing my frame, recycling me for scrap metal in a junkyard down the road. I will hear not only the sounds of my voice fading into the smoky air as they toss my wood into the incinerator, but also the sounds of men sweating and heaving my iron, crushing it into reusable pieces. It will be the end of me, you know.

STACCATO: It could be. But. You don't know that. Out of tune, yes. Broken keys. No longer the monument of perfection you were in your prime, I guess. *(chuckle)* But. He seems to like you. *(winks)* He's playing pretty well. Really knows. What he's doing, that is.

WOMAN: I don't know him. This is not my usual. The usual is the occasional chopsticks, the bored kid walking up, deciding he's a regular Bach, and giving me a pounding headache for the next thirty minutes. Who the hell needs to punch the keys on a piano. My F-sharp would like a word with him. I've been near computer labs before, heard them teach the youngsters, "You don't hit keys, you press them." Typing is one thing, a keyboard for twenty bucks, but my keys are worth thousands. Fragile. Treat 'em with care. Not everyone likes a massage from Hercules.

MARCATO: **Unless the song is about Hercules.**

WOMAN: Unless the song is about Hercules.

MARCATO: **Or it portrays the inimical advances of unwanted suitors.**

WOMAN: Yes, or that— I get it—

MARCATO: **It could also invoke the crashing fury of tempests.**

WOMAN: Thank you. I realize this is your area of expertise. I'm just saying it's not so friendly to the ole bag of bones as they stand right now. Where can I find someone to enjoy playing concertos and riveting solos? I'm fit for tinder right now and the world knows it. Shipped off to the junkyard in a week. I dreamed of once living with an eccentric artist, she sits inside drafting, scribbling, marking out, *scribbling*—

STACCATO: Scribble. Yes. But that's not all. They write. Test. Think. Dream. Talk. Hum. Weave. Tease. Pen. Doodle. Jot. Scrawl. Sing. Scream. Heave. Rock. Pace. Sit. Pace. Nibble. Breathe. Act. Reach. Grab. Smell. Squiggle. Scrabble. Squabble. Yell. Whisper. Laugh. Whistle. Pull. Sit. Reach. Touch. Play. That's the process.

MARCATO: **None come to press their heavy fingers into the worn keys. I grow sluggish through the ages. I need a new master, one in control. A player with finesse and ample substance behind their weathered digits. We all need it. Or else—**

WOMAN: I miss that. I really do. That long progression to completion. I remember playing for as long as it took until she had a completed work and we were so proud and it seemed like forever. I will never die so long as that can happen again and again and again and we can play...

(WOMAN looks at MAN playing. The man has been playing for the duration of this and seems frustrated by the lack of responsiveness from the piano. He has not given up and begins to play more furiously, passionately.)

WOMAN: My god, I feel alive. The dust is being thrown from my hammers and once again I am beautiful. I want it to last so much longer. Who are you? Never stop. Never stop playing.

// (STACCATO and MARCATO begin speaking their monologues simultaneously at this point, as the WOMAN walks to the piano and begins to sing. The song matches his animations. She sits next to the MAN at the piano until STACCATO and MARCATO finish their monologues.

STACCATO: //Never. Never stop. Don't stop. Playing. Keys. Forever. Lifelong. Hope. Rebirth. A new beginning. A chance. Don't. You can stay. With me. With us. Dancing. Prancing. Short. Snappy. Notes flipping. Trilling. On the wind. Endless. Infinite. On the waves. Swimming. Floating. Without bound. Interminable. Time everlasting. Never. Stop. No. Be there for me. Love? Attached. Distinct. Equal halves. Partners. You need me. You need us. Don't stop. Must. Play.

MARCATO: //**Never stop playing your song. You understand the strength that courses through your thickening veins as you play. Stand up and shout. Rejoice. Plant your feet with us and join us in the fearless rush of emotions that cease to end. Demonstrate the power of your youth and muscle through with the easy breath of your lungs upon your handiwork. Do not abscond with the force of your body and leave us to decay. You have the liveliness that we thrive upon, the spirited dynamism of your mind and will. Don't stop. Must. Play.**

(The WOMAN stops singing as the monologues end. The MAN looks up, astonished. He cannot bring himself to stop playing. He wants this moment to last forever.)

MAN: I stopped enjoying piano when I was twelve. My mother forced me to take lessons three times a week from one Mrs. Cranstedter, a hellish old woman from down the street. She had a particular way of walking that seemed to imitate or maybe spawn the way she talked. A kind of swaying, stuttering motion. The kind you see only in stop motion films. She'd walk up and say 'Have you be-en pr-acticing, young-uh man?' Never had a damn clue what she would tell me to do. Scales this, keys that. Maybe it was the correct way to learn. But it seemed as soon as it became a chore for me to do, it stopped being something I wanted to spend time doing.

(We hear scales, arpeggios, exercises emanate from the piano.)

I spent the better part of four years of my life under the reign of this woman being paid a modest fortune to teach me to learn. I was utterly resistant, y'know. Not really one to take directions well. I never had the patience for it either. The repetition was killing me slowly, driving me into the depths of a slow but thorough disdain and resentment towards this instrument in front of me. As my stubbornness grew, Mrs. Cranstedter became more determined to sit me in my bench for hours on end. It's a very similar principle to parents making their children eat their vegetables. It becomes a game of how long the parents are willing to put up with yelling at their kids, and, from the other side, how long the kid is willing to sit at the dinner table with their leafy greens in front of them when everybody else is watching tv in the other room. One day my overlord approached, sat on the bench with me, opened her book, and a scrap of paper fell out into my lap. I picked it up, looked at it, realized what it was. I saw lines, five lines, four spaces, dots, dashes, letters. It was a score. She asked for it back and I told her she had to play it first. She looked at me a good long minute before snatching this piece of paper back, shoving me over a few inches, and setting her hands in the ready position. I thought about it and I'll be damned if I had never seen her play before that point. It was magnificent. Contrary to my maulings of the keys, I heard what had been missing in my lessons. Drive? Creativity? Yeah, it was there. But there was also the idea of something new, something fresh, and something that will keep reviving in a different manner every time you play it. It's fucking unique, man.

(A song begins to play. It is a simple melody, old-fashioned, but catchy. It is only four measures long. It plays once and fades away.)

And that changed my entire perspective of the language. I became a star pupil as long as I was working on something new. Digging through the crisp unread material wasn't enough either. I had to discover and create new things myself. But the most interesting part was that the old things could become new with the touch of a new key, or a different tempo, or a change in rhythm. I challenged myself to reinvent the things I played. To repurpose them. Take the scraps and old and done and make it groundbreaking. And nothing ever gets old.

(MAN begins to close his song. He stands up, begins to walk out. WOMAN reenters the piano, followed by MARCATO and STACCATO. The lid closes and music finally plays. It is the same song that he learned from Mrs. Cranstedter. However, WOMAN has modified it. She replays the same melody from within the piano over and over in different ways, indescribably separate and new. The MAN returns to the piano and joins her in reworking the melodies. They finally close out the song, stand up, turn to audience, and bow. He turns back to the piano and begins to wheel it off-stage. He is taking it with him. Lights down.)

THE END

TONY DEL GROSSO *is a senior Theatre major at Transylvania University. He has performed in several Transylvania University plays including* Trust *and the student-written production* Today is History. *This is his second showcase as a playwright and he plans to continue developing his work.*

◆ ◆ ◆

Re-Contextualization

If we are to achieve a richer culture, rich in contrasting values, we must recognize the whole gamut of human potentialities, and so weave a less arbitrary social fabric, one in which each diverse human gift will find a fitting place.

– Margaret Mead, *Sex and Temperment in Three Primitive Societies*

In realistic productions, playwrights as storytellers are invisible to audiences, who relate primarily to characters on stage. What happens, then, when a storyteller becomes part of the storytelling, not merely as narrator but as active participant with an interpretive agenda? Furthermore, what happens when familiar stories from one culture are interpreted from outside that culture? This is re-contextualization – the re-location of perspective on narrative; the shift from an assumed "objective" playwright/observer to active participation in narration or interpretation by some other character, group, or culture.

Re-contextualization makes the familiar unfamiliar by examining it through an alternative lens. A good example is Tom Stoppard's *Rosencrantz and Guildenstern Are Dead,* which positions minor characters from *Hamlet* centerstage. In Stoppard's topsy-turvy approach, we no longer focus on Hamlet's struggle with his conscience or the King's usurpation of the throne, but rather, we follow two hapless young men struggling against a cosmic scheme that negates free will and seals their fate. Stoppard's existential comedy calls attention to aspects of the tragedy that Shakespeare did not explore in depth.

Another example is Timberlake Wertenbaker's *Our Country's Good,* in which British prisoners in 18ᵗʰ century Australia mount a production of George Farquhar's Restoration comedy, *The Recruiting Officer.* The leader's purpose is to boost general morale in difficult circumstances, but their storytelling leads to larger questions about the possibility of redemption and the transforming powers of theatre, both of which are central concerns to the prisoners, though they probably weren't to Farquhar.

New interpretations of classic literature, historical events, and cultural myths can disclose significant differences amongst individuals and groups. Take *Amadeus*, for instance: Salieri's description of an unruly Mozart is surely informed more by envy than an obligation to biographical accuracy. Moreover, when a classic is re-presented by an underprivileged group, the performance can't help but engage in the politics of disenfranchisement and exclusion. And a play whose title alone suggests the politics of its interpretation of historical events is *The Persecution and Assassination of Jean-Paul Marat, as Performed by the Inmates of the Asylum of Charenton Under the Direction of the Marquis de Sade.*

Re-contextualization also underscores the relativity of human existence; no two individuals or groups experience any single event in the same way. When differing worldviews collide on stage, the illusion of objectivity, which provides a foundation for assumptions of realism, vanishes. In a subjective universe, the reporting or retelling of events emphasizes the psychology or psychopathology of the narrator. When adding an outside perspective to a dramatic narrative, playwrights are well advised to embrace the ambiguities of unreliability and suspense of unpredictability in their choice of narrators.

WORKSHOP: RE-CONTEXTUALIZATION

How does one group understand and reimagine the stories of another? This workshop zeroes in on conflicts that can arise when the narratives and agendas of different cultures collide. In this workshop writers filter dramatic events from a classic through the perspective of a person or group other than the main characters in the original play. The narrator(s) should be actively involved and deeply affected in some way by the content of the classic. In other words, there's good reason the person or group is reinterpreting the play, and the stakes of their retelling should be high.

Step 1: **Selection.** Each writer selects a well-known play and brings a copy to class. They'll want to write on and possibly cut up the text, so it's best to use duplicated copies rather than published scripts. Next, identify a group affected by the action or theme of the play but a group not represented in the cast (perhaps future generations, a community downstream, lower or upper classes, etc.).

Step 2: **Pre-Writing.** Ask writers to think of reasons or occasions when the outsider(s) would perform the play, only reinterpreted to convey their side of the story. Next, identify individual characters (members of the group) who will perform the play. Are there direct correlations or contrasts between performer/characters and characters in the play (e.g., are women performing an all-male play? Are children playing adult roles?)? Finally, identify three details or outcomes in the original about which the original's author and group could disagree.

Step 3: **Write the Play.** Write a scene or, if the original is short or can be shortened (that may be part of the interpretation), an entirely new version of the original as reimagined by the characters/people who perform it.

Step 4: **Read the Play.** Read the plays aloud in class. This activity works best if writers bring enough copies so that everyone reading a role has a script and the playwright (and others) can listen.

Step 5: **Discussion.** How does the revision differ from the original? If the two versions differ significantly, which do you believe? Can the audience follow the content of the original as well as the intentions and changes in the adaptation? Does the reason the characters are performing the play influence your response to their performance? How does the revised play affect your understanding of the original? Is the revision as timely and relevant as the original?

◆◆◆

PLAYWRIGHT PERSPECTIVE:
Sheila Callaghan

"The rules are built as the play unfolds; not before the house lights go down."

Why have you incorporated non-realistic theatrical elements into your plays – what has it contributed, required or allowed?

I've found in my own writing that opening up the imaginative landscape of the play provokes a disorientation in the audience, which allows it to engage on a different, unique level with the work. Breaking with realism encourages a shifting dialogue between the observers and the observed, the expectations of which revolve around the act of constructing meaning rather than the passive consumption of information. The play itself invites its audience into the psychic space of the world, where the rules are built as the play unfolds; not before the house lights go down.

Where did (or do) you find inspiration for non-realistic elements in your plays?

For me, the play finds the form. While writing *Crumble (Lay Me Down, Justin Timberlake)* I was living in a terrible NYC apartment with a banging radiator and a crumbling ceiling and a malevolent plumbing system. The apartment loomed large in my psyche, so large that it became a personified masculine adversary. So of course, he showed up in the play I was writing. This is an example of the external being internalized and then spewed back out as an entity in my writing. But for *That Pretty Pretty; or, The Rape Play,* I was writing with a lot of aggressive, frantic, fragmented energy, and I wanted the play's form to reflect this. The result is a jerking in and out of time, and a fundamental irreverence for the prescribed rules of realism. And in my play *Lascivious Something*, I set out to write a realistic play, but I found myself unable to tell the story without exploring the subconscious desires of my characters, which resulted in a hiccupping structure that doubles back and retells the same moments with different results. In general, my baseline tends to be rooted in the logical and emotional truths of the characters and situations (which simulate "realism"), and once that is established, the work detonates itself in any number of ways.

> *Does the opportunity to incorporate non-realistic elements in your plays allow you to explore dimensions of the human condition or tell other kinds of stories than the conventions of realism allow?*

Yes. Absolutely. For me, realism only allows for the lies. They are beautiful lies, but often they are suspect.

SHEILA CALLAGHAN'S *plays have been produced and developed with Soho Rep, Playwright's Horizons, The LARK, Actors Theatre of Louisville, New Georges, and Woolly Mammoth, and internationally in New Zealand, Australia, Norway, Germany, Portugal, and the Czech Republic. Sheila is the recipient of the Princess Grace Award, a Jerome Fellowship, a Cherry Lane Mentorship Fellowship, the Susan Smith Blackburn Award, and the Whiting Award. Sheila is an affiliated artist with Clubbed Thumb, a resident of New Dramatists, and a member of the Obie-winning playwright's organization 13P. In 2010, Callaghan was profiled by* Marie Claire *as one of "18 Successful Women Who Are Changing the World." That year she was also named one of* Variety's *"10 Screenwriters to Watch."*

◆ ◆ ◆

Bricolage, or Pastiche

The nitrogen in our DNA, the calcium in our teeth, the iron in our blood, the carbon in our apple pies were made in the interiors of collapsing stars. We are made of starstuff... If you wish to make an apple pie from scratch, you must first invent the universe.

– Carl Sagan, *Cosmos*

A "bricolage" is a construction developed from whatever materials happen to be available. The term "collage" refers to a similar technique, something postmodernists also call "pastiche." Whichever term is preferred, one feature that's useful for playwrights is the limitation of source material; that's an integral feature of bricolage. So for now, bricolage it is.

Here are two examples of how we experience the world as a bricolage. Writing for the *New York Times* in 1995, Bernard Sharratt called the Internet "a global bricolage," and Susan Strasser wrote in *Waste and Want: A Social History of Trash*, "Cooking with leftovers was bricolage – a dialogue between the cook and the available materials."

Whether working with computers, leftovers, or actors, the point of bricolage is to create a compelling whole by sequencing and juxtaposing disconnected bits of culture. This artistic form mirrors our daily experience as we confront thousands of images and bits of information. On stage, bricolage celebrates variety and thrives on theatrical energy generated when disparate shards of culture collide like flints, sparking flashes of absurdity and meanings that puzzle and delight. As artistic expression, bricolage can reference anything, which is why limited source material helps provide thematic cohesion.

Contemporary playwrights who create by bricolage are Charles L. Mee and JoAnne Akalaitis, both of whom defy mainstream or *avant-garde* categorization. Mee's *Under Construction* is a bricolage of literature, music, and visual arts. That theatrical assemblage charts the progression of American culture as seen through the work

91

of artists from the 1940s to present day. Akalaitis constructed a bricolage text titled *Ti Jean Blues* from numerous literary works by and about Jack Kerouac, which she then mixed with 1950s dance and the music of Philip Glass and Billie Holiday. While it evokes the random encounters of daily "reality," bricolage obviously does not conform to conventions of realism. It doesn't rely on cause and effect, character development, or Aristotle. It exists on a moment-to-moment basis, and only by taking the ride can you understand the journey.

How is drama sustained when plot and character no longer provide the primary organizing principles of theatrical experience? This workshop explores theatrical possibilities of layered and fragmented cultural collisions.

WORKSHOP: BRICOLAGE

A play composed in bricolage pieces together ideas and expressions rather than following a linear series of events that are determined by plot and characters. In this workshop writers create an overall theatrical experience comprised of disparate moments that might be musical, literary, dramatic, poetic, photographic, movement- or spectacle-based, to name a few possibilities.

Step 1: **Selection.** Writers bring to the workshop three pieces of literature, a piece of music, and a visual image. The literary selections should represent three different genres: fiction, non-fiction, poetry, drama, journalism, cookbooks, comics, instructional guides, travelogues, letters, diaries.

Step 2: **Pre-Writing.** The next steps familiarize playwrights with their texts, music, and visual image. Do the following analyses in five-minute increments. Summarize each piece of literature in a sentence or paragraph. Describe the music and visual image in a sentence or paragraph. Identify themes and ideas in each artifact. Name the characters who speak or sing, or are the speakers the authors and composer/lyricist themselves? Are there characters in the image? Finally, circle ten favorite passages in the texts.

Step 3: **Composition/Writing.** Select one artifact (text, music, or image) to provide an overall structure (beginning, middle, end). Think of this as an organizing principle or a skeleton upon which you'll distribute selections from other works. Now, begin to piece together a sequence of theatrical moments. It may be easiest to cut and arrange pieces of the text and music/lyrics so you can clearly see the juxtapositions and progression. Where and how does the image fit into the overall event (as a staged moment, visual background, character in the play, concluding image, memory)? Use at least three passages from each literary source – the length of the passage doesn't matter, but revisiting each text provides motifs and continuity. Because writers will have questions, it's good to start this process in the workshop; writers can finesse and polish their bricolage play later. Type all the pieces into a single document in script form. If there are no characters in the traditional sense, only speakers or voices, writers can identify them as Actor 1, Actor 2, etc.

Step 4: **Read.** Read the plays aloud. This works best when writers bring enough copies so that everyone reading a role has a script and the playwright (and others) can listen. Pass around the image and play the music at the appropriate moments during the reading.

Step 5: **Discuss.** What are the playwrights' overall impressions of each piece? What aspect of each play did they like best? Least? Why? How do the texts and artifacts dialogue with one another? Is the organizing principle effective – was there a journey or progression from beginning to end? How does the bricolage compare with more conventional realistic plays in terms of moment-to-moment interest, surprise, suspense, complexity?

◆ ◆ ◆

BRICOLAGE PLAY

In the following bricolage play by Harold N. Cropp, the lines are footnoted to indicate how the source texts are juxtaposed and interwoven. Because interpretations of copyright law vary regarding texts brought into dialogue with one another in this way, it's safest to use material that has fallen out of copyright or get permission from the authors if the material is to be performed. For that reason, contemporary dramatic texts are not often incorporated into bricolage or devised work. However, there is a playwright who invites others to sample his work for their own bricolage constructions: Charles L. Mee. He creates and shares his work on-line under the rubric "the (re) making project," and here he explains his philosophy and policy.

> Please feel free to take the plays from this website and use them freely as a resource for your own work: that is to say, don't just make some cuts or rewrite a few passages or re-arrange them or put in a few texts that you like better, but pillage the plays as I have pillaged the structures and contents of the plays of Euripides and Brecht and stuff out of Soap Opera Digest and the evening news and the internet, and build your own, entirely new, piece – and then, please, put your own name to the work that results.
>
> But, if you would like to perform the plays essentially or substantially as I have composed them, they are protected by copyright in the versions you read here, and you need to clear performance rights.

For further information about Charles Mee's theories on originality, culture, and (re)making, as well as the texts of all his dramatic works, visit his website: www.charlesmee.org.

Odyssey Across America: a bricolage
by Harold N. Cropp

*(Lights come up on a projection of an Abelardo
Morrell tent camera photograph, "Tent-Camera
Image on Ground: View of Rio Grande and Mexico
Near Boquillas Canyon, Big Bend National Park,
Texas, 2011." In the semi-darkness, we hear Leo
Kottke "Last Steam Train Engine." Lights come
up on three stools, each in its own pool of light.
On the stools are three actors: Peter, Homer/Man
1, and Coop/Woman 1).*

WOMAN: Peter, where is north?[1]

PETER: After one semester of living together...I was nine-
teen and on one sweet summer's day in 1971, we were
married[2]

MAN: North? North is there, my love. The brook runs
west.[3]

PETER: Why not just leave this American scene and head
for another country?... We Americans were blowing up
anything and everyone for no clear reason in Vietnam.[4]

WOMAN: The rest, all those who had perdition 'scaped
By war or on the Deep, dwelt now at home[5]

PETER: When our marriage disintegrated, I realized one
sure thing. I knew I was going to have to get my head
together and I would have to do it by myself.[6]

MAN: What in the world do ya think yer a doin' hikin' in
this blizzard?[7]

WOMAN: Muse make the man thy theme, for shrewdness
famed
And genius versatile, who far and wide
A Wand'rer, after Ilium overthrown,
Discover'd various cities, and the mind
And manners learn'd of men, in lands remote.[8]

MAN: Pete, what are you still doing in Alfred?[9]

WOMAN: West running brook then call it.[10]

PETER: I've decided to leave this godforsaken country and
try somewhere else.[11]

MAN: If you want to leave, go right ahead, but first you sure as shootin' ought to give this country a chance.[12]

WOMAN: Our fix'd resolve, that brave Ulysses thence
Depart, uncompanied by God or man.
Borne on a corded raft, and suff'ring woe
Extreme, he on the twentieth day shall reach,
Not sooner, Scherie the deep-soil'd, possess'd
By the Phæacians, kinsmen of the Gods.[13]

PETER: When I got home from work that summer day, I called Cooper and we went for a long meditative walk. Stu's words were like a neon sign flashing on and off. After five or six miles, they finally broke through my mule-thick head.[14]

WOMAN: Go on. You thought of something.[15]

PETER: I made a decision about what we would do. Cooper and I were going to walk across the U.S.A.[16]

MAN: who bid'st me pass
The perilous gulph of Ocean on a raft,
That wild expanse terrible, which even ships
Pass not, though form'd to cleave their way with ease,
And joyful in propitious winds from Jove.[17]

WOMAN: What does it think it's doing running west
when all the other country brooks flow east
to reach the ocean?[18]

PETER: Cooper and I were training...there were rocks everywhere, my feet and ankles were so hard, I didn't have to concentrate on them. Instead, I looked straight ahead, yearning for the river at the bottom of the hill that Cooper and I would swim across. Suddenly, Cooper darted in front of me...[19]

WOMAN: nudged him to the side and grabbed a thick copperhead in (my) mouth. With one vicious, tearing shake,...[20]

PETER: he killed the snake that I would have stepped on and that would have bitten me for sure.[21]

MAN: It must be the brook can trust itself to go by contraries[22]

WOMAN: The way I can with you – and you with me –

Because we're – we're – I don't know what we are.
What are we?[23]

PETER: Cooper and I were alone and the long walk had
begun.[24]

WOMAN: We must be something.
We've said we two. Let's change that to we three.
As you and I are married to each other,
We'll both be married to the brook.[25]

MAN: Chatham Hill was a tiny town. If you want to meet
someone real, and a character, you've got to meet Homer
Davenport, the greatest mountain man alive.[26]

WOMAN: Homer sure can be unfriendly! Guess that's why
he lives up there.[27]

MAN: He don't like people much.[28]

WOMAN: Look, look, it's waving to us with a wave
To let us know it hears me.[29]

MAN: (cackling) Hey don't let all my nonsense scare ya from
goin'to pay a visit to old Homer. With you a-walkin', and yer
beard, and that dawg, Homer might take a likin to ya.[30]

WOMAN: Alas! I tremble lest some God design
T' ensnare me yet, bidding me quit the raft.
But let me well beware how I obey
Too soon that precept, for I saw the land
Of my foretold deliv'rance far remote.[31]

PETER: We started walking while it was still half dark…At
the end of the pavement, a deeply rutted, frozen red dirt
road began…We headed up. After two miles the steep-
ness leveled off, and…I saw an old log cabin…As I was
trying to open the decrepit gate…[32]

MAN: What do you want, boy?[33]

WOMAN: It wasn't waved to us.
It wasn't, yet it was[34]

PETER: Are you Homer Davenport ?[35]

MAN: No, I ain't. Homer lives about three miles further
up the mountain. I'm his only neighbor, and my name's
Douglas Allison. Lived right here for my sixty-two years.
In this cabin for forty. Yes, sir! I was born right here. I'm
gonna die here.[36]

WOMAN: Here we, in our impatience of the steps,
Get back to the beginning of beginnings[37]

PETER: Back on the narrow red-dirt road, we walked for
about another half mile, and then Homer's dirt sidewalk
turned into a rock-scattered stream...Ten muddy miles
had passed before I saw a bend in the stream bank.[38]

WOMAN: Nothing ever scared (me)...but this time (I) crept
over and let out (a) hair curling growl[39]

PETER: Slowly I lifted my head. Fifty feet away stood an
ageless old man whose flowing white hair and beard
glowed with life.[40]

MAN: Now, what'd you say you were up to?[41]

PETER: Peter Jenkins and that's Cooper and we're walking
across the U.S.A.[42]

WOMAN: the Sirens sitting in the meads
Charm with mellifluous song, while all around
The bones accumulated lie of men
Now putrid, and the skins mould'ring away.[43]

PETER: Our life runs down in sending up the clock.[44]

MAN: In (my) kitchen, (I) moved with a grace that could
match that of a chef in the best restaurant in New York...
Git ya one of them straightened coat hangers and cook
yerself a chop o' meat.[45]

WOMAN: First shalt thou reach the Sirens; they the hearts
Enchant of all who on their coast arrive[46]

PETER: Homer's way of life made all my suburban blab
seem dumb and meaningless.[47]

WOMAN: Some say existence...forever in one place, stands
still and dances, but it runs away.[48]

MAN: One thing I've learned is that ya never know what's
gonna happen to ya in this old life...Ya know what you
should do? You ought to settle down here...I'll teach ya
all the ways of livin'up here and someday when ya get
a place built, you can have yerself a family.[49]

WOMAN: But as for thee – thou hear them if thou wilt.
Yet let thy people bind thee to the mast
Erect, encompassing thy feet and arms
With cordage well-secured to the mast-foot,

So shalt thou, raptur'd, hear the Sirens' song.[50]
MAN: It seriously, sadly, runs away
To fill the abyss's void with emptiness.[51]
PETER: Homer...Maybe Cooper and I will come back here
to live with you on your mountain. Tomorrow, though,
we're going to walk on across the country.[52]
WOMAN: It flows beside us in this water brook,
But it flows over us.[53]
PETER: After I crossed the Cahaba River, I was rolling
through Shelby County. That was the night I met the
"Shelby County Drunk Four."[54]
WOMAN: Thence, o'er the Deep proceeding sad, we
reach'd
The land at length, where, giant-sized and free
From all constraint of law, the Cyclops dwell.[55]
PETER: The dimly lit phone booth stood alone in the darkest
corner of the gravel lot...As...I talked...a slow-moving
green pick-up drove up. The pick-up turned off its lights
and parked right in front of me.[56]
WOMAN: Here dwelt a giant vast, who far remote
His flocks fed solitary, converse none
Desiring, sullen, savage, and unjust.[57]
PETER: A man got out on the driver's side and started over
to the booth...The unsteady man was big and looked
in his late forties. His khaki work clothes were coated
with cinderblock dust and cement and his bloated hairy
stomach leaked out between bulging buttons.[58]
WOMAN: Who are ye, strangers? from what distant shore
Roam ye the waters? traffic ye? or bound
To no one port, wander, as pirates use,
At large the Deep, exposing life themselves,
And enemies of all mankind beside?[59]
MAN: Where you from, you ugly whiskered hippie?[60]
PETER: Connecticut...I'm walking across America.[61]
MAN: Hear that boys? This liar wants us ta believe he's
a-walkin cross America.[62]
PETER: The men in the truck laughed meaner than any laugh
I had ever heard.[63]

MAN: I'm gonna break ever' bone in yer slimy body, you freak! Yer down here fer drug dealin' and I'm gonna kill ya before ya get ar youngins.[64]

WOMAN: I thus replied.

Since we reach, at last,
Thy knees, we beg such hospitable fare,
Or other gift, as guests are wont to obtain.
Illustrious lord! respect the Gods, and us
Thy suitors; suppliants are the care of Jove
The hospitable; he their wrongs resents
And where the stranger sojourns, there is he.[65]

PETER: What makes you so brave? This fight's not fair! What happens when I whip you? You're so brave 'cause all of your friends in the truck, and if I got you down they'd all jump out and that'd be it for me...You know something...Everyone up North and throughout the rest of the country expects something like this to happen to a Yankee walking across Alabama. If you beat me up, I'll have to write about you and that will ruin all the good things that have happened to me in your state.[66]

WOMAN: Cyclops! thou hast my noble name enquired,
Which I will tell thee. Give me, in return,
The promised boon, some hospitable pledge.
My name is Outis, Outis I am call'd
At home, abroad; wherever I am known.[67]

MAN: Yankee boy, ya knew right along I was tryin'ta pick a fight. Ya see, my boy's hooked on them drugs "n" been thataway since he got back from Vietnam.[68]

WOMAN: What grievous hurt hath caused thee,
Polypheme!
Thus yelling to alarm the peaceful ear
Of night, and break our slumbers?...
Them answer'd, then, Polypheme from his cave.
Oh, friends! I die! and Outis gives the blow.
To whom with accents wing'd his friends without.
If no man harm thee, but thou art alone,
And sickness feel'st, it is the stroke of Jove,
And thou must bear it;[69]

MAN: I aimed ta whip you good 'cause I figured ya were
one a' them drug pushers. Come on over to tha truck,
boy. We gotta have a beer tagether.[70]

PETER: It flows between us, over us, and *with* us.
And it is time, strength, tone, light, life, and love.[71]

WOMAN: And even substance lapsing unsubstantial;
The universal cataract of death
That spends to nothingness – and unresisted[72]

PETER: The semi-sized truck had a tank full of water to be
delivered around the Farm...Always in control, Cooper
ran along the two foot bank beside the weaving, bounc-
ing truck. He wouldn't let the truck travel by, but leaped
down off the bank, right under the rear...the whole truck
lurched and went over a big bump.[73]

MAN: Argus the while,
Ulysses' dog, uplifted where he lay
His head and ears erect. Ulysses him
Had bred long since, himself, but rarely used,
Departing, first, to Ilium. Him the youths
In other days led frequent to the chase
Of wild goat, hart and hare; but now he lodg'd
A poor old cast-off, of his Lord forlorn[74]

PETER: I knew it was Cooper under those wheels. He could
survive even if his body had taken the entire weight of
the truck. He was forever. Nothing could hurt him.[75]

WOMAN: There lay, with dog-devouring vermin foul
All over, Argus; soon as he perceived
Long-lost Ulysses nigh, down fell his ears
Clapp'd close, and with his tail glad sign he gave
Of gratulation, impotent to rise
And to approach his master as of old.[76]

PETER: I knew Coops would wake up any minute from
being knocked unconscious and want to play or chase a
stick... Hurry! Get over here, doc! Tell me quick! Will
it help to get my dog to a doctor? I think he's knocked
out or in a coma![77]

WOMAN: Then his destiny released
Old Argus, soon as he had lived to see
Ulysses in the twentieth year restored.[78]

101

MAN: I'm sorry but your dog is dead.[79]

WOMAN: Our life runs down in sending up the clock.
The brook runs down in sending up our life.
The sun runs down in sending up the brook.
And there is something sending up the sun.[80]

PETER: After walking from Alfred, New York to the Gulf
Coast, I moved into Lipsey Hall...Something happened
a few days later that changed my life and my walk forever. ..the students were having a party and Bill asked
me to go...scanning the room full of proper preachers
and students, I saw her.[81]

WOMAN: So saying, she left her chamber, musing much
In her descent, whether to interrogate
Her Lord apart, or whether to imprint,
At once, his hands with kisses and his brows.
O'erpassing light the portal-step of stone
She enter'd. He sat opposite, illumed
By the hearth's sprightly blaze[82]

PETER: We fell in love and everything got closer to
heavenly.[83]

MAN: It was mid-October when things went wrong...
volcanic love began to cool along with the weather and
winter breezes from the Gulf that made the pecan trees
drop their golden fruit all over campus.[84]

WOMAN: Oh, if you take it off to lady-land,
As't were the country of the Amazons...[85]

PETER: Those cool winds and the reality of what lay ahead
sobered Barbara. She realized for the first time that if we
got married she would have to walk the rest of the way
across America with me.[86]

WOMAN: Let's change that to we three.
As you and I are married to each other,
We'll both be married to the brook.[87]

MAN: Reverend Charles Green...told us Mom Beall
had come all the way from Detroit to speak a special
message...[88]

WOMAN: The old and wise lady began to tell us a story
from the Old Testament...about Abraham and his son,

Isaac…Abraham…sent his best servant to Mesopotamia..
to have a wife from there…Rebekah came to the well…
the servant knew this was the girl for Isaac…he followed
her home.[89]

MAN: Rebekah's family called her to them…Will you go
with this man…Will you go with this man…one last
time…will you go with this man?[90]

PETER: So welcome in her eyes Ulysses seem'd,
Around whose neck winding her snowy arms,
She clung as she would loose him never more.[91]

WOMAN: Peter, I'll go with you.[92]

ALL: It is this backward motion toward the source,
Against the stream, that most we see ourselves in,
The tribute of the current to the source.
It is from this in nature we are from.
It is most us.[93]

> *(Lights slowly down on the actors, leaving the
> image of Morrell's tent camera up as the strains
> of Leo Kottke's version of "Living in the Country"
> come up and as the sound and image fade slowly
> to black.)*

END OF PLAY

HAROLD N. CROPP *is now in his twenty-second season with
the Commonweal Theatre Company, where he has been in
a leadership position since 1994. His plays include* Vandals, Preachers, and Tellers of Tales; A Country Christmas; Robin Goodfellow; *adaptations of Ibsen's* Ghosts
and The Wild Duck; *and the ten-minute play,* Nicholas
Cage Is Not His Real Name. *He received his B.A. from
Brown, his M.B.A. from Santa Clara University, and his
M.F.A. in acting from the National Theatre Conservatory
in Denver. Hal currently serves as Executive Director of
the Commonweal.*

ENDNOTES

1-Robert Frost, "West Running Brook," p.170, *New Enlarged Anthology of Robert Frost's Poems*, Washington Square Press, 1971
2-Peter Jenkins, *A Walk Across America*, p.20, William Morrow & Company, Inc., 1979
3-Frost, op.cit.
4-Jenkins, op.cit. p.22
5-Homer, op.cit.
6-Jenkins, op.cit., p.21
7-Jenkins, op.cit. p.12
8-Homer, *The Odyssey,* William Cowper, trans., Gutenberg Press
9-Jenkins, op.cit. p.23
10-Frost, op.cit.
11-Jenkins, op.cit.p.23
12-ibid.
13-Homer, op.cit.
14-Jenkins op.cit. p.24
15-Frost, op.cit.
16-Jenkins, op.cit. p.24
17-Homer op.cit.
18 -Frost op.cit.
19-Jenkins, op.cit. p.14
20-ibid.
21-Ibid.
22-Frost op.cit.
23-Ibid.
24-Jenkins op.cit. p.33
25-Frost, op.cit.
26-Jenkins, op.cit.p.67
27-ibid.
28-Ibid.
29-Frost, op.cit.
30-Jenkins, op.cit. p.68
31-Homer, op.cit.
32-Jenkins, op.cit. p.69
33-ibid.
34-Frost op.cit.
35-Jenkins, op.cit. p.69
36-Ibid.
37-Frost, op.cit.
38-Jenkins, op.cit. p.70
39-Ibid.
40-Jenkins, op.cit. P.70
41-ibid.p.71
42-ibid.
43-Homer, op.cit.
44-Frost, op.cit.
45-Jenkins, op.cit. p.74
46-Homer, op.cit.
47-Jenkins, op.cit. p.75
48-Frost, op.cit.
49-Jenkins, op.cit. p.78
50-Homer, op.cit.
51-Frost, op.cit.
52-Jenkins, op.cit. p.80
53-Frost, op.cit.
54-Jenkin, op.cit. p.219
55-Homer, op.cit.
56-Jenkins, op.cit.p.220
57-Homer, op.cit.
58-Jenkins, op.cit. p.221
59-Homer, op.cit.
60-Jenkins, op.cit.
61-ibid.
62-ibid.
63-Ibid.
64-Ibid.
65-Homer, op.cit.
66-Jenkins, op.cit. p.222
67-Homer, op.cit.
68-Jenkins, op.cit. p.222
69-Homer, op.cit.
70-Jenkins, op.cit. p.223
71-Frost, op.cit.
72-ibid.
73-Jenkins, op.cit.p.208
74-Homer, op.cit.
75-Jenkins. Op.cit. p.208
76-Homer, op.cit.
77-Jenkins, op.cit. p.209
78-Homer, op.cit.
79-Jenkins, op.cit. p.209
80-Frost, op.cit.
81-Jenkins, op.cit. p.270-271
82-Homer, op.cit.
83-Jenkins, op.cit. p.279
84-Ibid.
85-Frost, op.cit.
86-Jenkins, op.cit. p.278
87-Frost, op.cit.
88-Jenkins, op.cit. p.284
89- Ibid.
90-ibid.
91-Homer, op.cit.
92-Jenkins, op.cit. p.286
93-Frost, op.cit.

Virtuosity

The attraction of the virtuoso for the public is very like that of the circus for the crowd. There is always the hope that something dangerous will happen.
– Claude Debussy, *Monsieur Croche, the Dilettante Hater*

How much are playwrights asking of actors, directors, and designers? Realistic plays require actors to behave and emote like actual people with whom audiences can identify and empathize. The methodologies of realistic acting, beginning with Konstantin Stanislavski and later adapted by founders of the Actors Studio, emphasize emotional recall, motivation, and action. During the 20th century, a synchronicity in playwriting, acting, and audience expectation occurred so that the most celebrated plays were almost always exemplars of realism: *A Raisin in the Sun*, *The Crucible*, *Steel Magnolias*, *Burn This*, *Crimes of the Heart*, *Fences*, *The Heidi Chronicles*, *Doubt*.

In her book, *Making Art in an Unpredictable World*, director Anne Bogart speculates as to why realism became the dominant form in American playwriting.

Mainstream American theater criticism is geared toward a playwright's ability to stimulate empathy. It is then no coincidence that the majority of contemporary American playwrights concentrate their energy and imagination on creating empathy above all other possible attractions that the theater can provide. Not encouraged by the critical establishment to consider spectacle, alchemy, participation, ritual, or education, the writers assume that the theater is predominantly a vehicle for empathy.

Appearing to speak and behave naturally within the dramaturgical structures of a realistic play is no small feat unto itself, and most playwrights don't ask much more of actors. The same holds true for challenges that playwrights present to designers.

That means that a lot of potential acting and design talent lies fallow. Have you ever read the special skills section of an actor's resume? Some play musical instruments and dance while others have acrobatic and circus skills. Some can in-line skate like pros, and others can solve a Rubik's cube in less than a minute. A few combine unusual talents in unique ways: playing the accordion while riding a unicycle and reciting text by Kafka.

Since these theatrical moments impress, delight, or even amaze, why don't playwrights incorporate more special skills into their scripts? Perhaps they fear that producers won't find actors with the necessary talents, but those days are gone or at least they are going fast.

Here are a few examples of playwrights and directors who've taken advantage of actors' multiple talents. Andrew Lloyd Webber's musical *Starlight Express* required actors to sing while in-line roller-skating around a three-story set. Director John Doyle cast musical productions on Broadway with actors who played instruments while singing and moving about, making other orchestral accompaniment unnecessary. And in *June Bride*, solo performer/playwright Sarah Felder escaped from a straightjacket while balancing on a bongo board and talking on a landline phone with the phone cord wrapped around her body. Felder's impossible feat provided a compelling metaphor for her character's emotional crisis – she was seeking parental approval for her lesbian marriage, but her father hung up and ended the call. Like the other examples listed here, Felder's intricate escape act – accompanied by a rousing audience rendition of "You Are My Sunshine" – became the production's climactic and most memorable event.

WORKSHOP: VIRTUOSITY

This workshop encourages playwrights to think outside the box of naturalistic behavior and colloquial speech; to imagine instead a performer's other talents and skills that could theatricalize a conflict and energize a production.

Step 1: **Dramatic conflict**. Ask writers to think of a basic dramatic situation: a character with an action and several obstacles that will create complications and conflict. Writers read these capsule descriptions aloud, then put them aside.

Step 2: **Brainstorm**. As a group or individually, writers list special skills (verbal, physical, artistic, athletic, magical, etc.) they have or know of.

Step 3: **Select**. Playwrights select from their lists a special skill that provides a metaphor for the character's challenge or conflict in the scenes they described.

Step 4: **Write**. Write a scene in which the character employs this special skill as he or she confronts the obstacles. (Note: the character needn't be accomplished at the skill – the very act of attempting the skill compels interest and failure can provide a moving lesson about human endeavor.)

Step 5: **Read**. Be sure to read stage directions along with the dialogue, since it's likely that much of the action involving the skill will be described.

Step 6: **Discuss**. How does the special skill add interest, color the action or tactics, contribute to dialogue, enhance metaphor? Did the use of one or more special skills become the main event or attraction of the scene? Consider the scene without the special skill – what is gained or lost?

◆ ◆ ◆

Playwright Perspective:
Naomi Iizuka

"The nature of human experience, whether it be devastating loss or awe-struck wonder, often eludes the vocabulary and conventions of realism."

There's an assignment that I often give playwriting students who are just beginning to write plays. I ask them to write an unstageable stage direction. I dare them to write the most impossible moment to stage, something that defies all known rules of space and time. I tell them not to worry about how a director and designers will pull it off. I tell them an unstageable stage direction is an invitation to all your collaborators to be as inventive, evocative, and surprising as possible. It is a message in a bottle that you send down the river to your collaborators and your audiences. It is a window into both the vast and infinitesimal mysteries of the universe as well as of the human heart.

There's nothing wrong with plays that tell stories in realistic ways (and by "realistic," I mean what we have come to accept as the conventions of realistic theatre). However, I'm of the belief that what really happens in life, how people really are, what we experience as reality, even what we know of how our natural universe really functions, is far more non-realistic than the conventions of theatrical realism would have us believe. We don't always have the language or the faculties to make sense of the things that happen to us. The nature of human experience, whether it be devastating loss or awe-struck wonder, often eludes the vocabulary and conventions of realism.

An unstageable direction, for me, is a metaphor for any non-realistic theatrical element. It is a reminder of the possibilities of live theatre. It is the antithesis of realism. At its best, it is the embodiment of some deeper mystery of our human experience. It is a wake-up call to our senses and our imaginations. It shakes us free of the familiar. It puts into a fleshy, material form fragments from our dreams, intuitions, ancient memories. It tantalizes and provokes us. It gives us solace.

When I think about the unstageable stage directions I have written over the years, I realize that many of them involve finding the language to come to terms with the fact of mortality, that we will all of us die, that our loved ones will die. In my play *Polaroid Stories*, a homeless girl turns into a star in the night sky at the moment of her death. I remember one university production of the play, in particular, where the actress wrapped herself in Christmas lights almost as though she were wrapping herself in a burial shroud, then scaled a ladder on the back wall of the darkened theatre. When she got to the top of the ladder, the Christmas lights that she had wrapped around herself clicked on. In a world of violence and chaos, it was this moment of astonishing beauty in a field of darkness that lingered long after everything else faded away.

The non-realistic element of an unstageable stage direction allows for the world to open up in a way that would never otherwise happen. It's as though a secret door opens and we're allowed entry into another world, a parallel universe that co-exists side by side with our own. In my play *Concerning Strange Devices From The Distant West*, time doesn't function in any remotely linear way. The play is a triptych. The first part takes place in Meiji-era Japan. The second part takes place in modern-day Tokyo. The third part takes place in a world that is both future and past, where the living and the dead coexist side by side, trying in some way to make sense of their lives. In the last moments of the play, an American woman long dead speaks to us from the vantage point of a ghost. She doesn't have the answers, but her very presence, how alive she seems, her incongruous joy, is what you remember more than words. In some ways, I realize that this is what I am trying to do in most all of my unstageable directions and in much of my writing: to bring to life ghosts, to give them human form, to make them visible, to give them a voice. At its heart, the unstageable stage direction is, for me, about bringing something or someone back to life. It's about defying that most basic fact of mortality, if only for a few moments on stage.

NAOMI IIZUKA'S *plays include* 36 Views, Strike-Slip, Anon(ymous), At the Vanishing Point, Polaroid Stories, Language of Angels, War of the Worlds *(in collaboration with Anne Bogart and SITI Company),* Tattoo Girl *and* Skin. *Her plays have been produced by Actors Theatre of Louisville, Berkeley Repertory Theater, the Joseph Papp Public Theatre/New York Shakespeare Festival, the Kennedy Center for Performing Arts, and the Brooklyn Academy of Music's "Next Wave Festival." Iizuka is a recipient of a PEN/Laura Pels Award, an Alpert Award, a Joyce Foundation Award, a Whiting Writers' Award, a Stavis Award, a Rockefeller Foundation MAP grant, an NEA/TCG Artist-in-Residence grant, a McKnight Fellowship, and a PEN Center USA West Award for Drama.*

◆◆◆

Extreme Symbolism

I think we're still in a muddle with our language, because once you get words and a spoken language it gets harder to communicate.
— Jane Goodall, *"Jane Goodall On Why Words Hurt,"*
Forbes.com

Whether they contribute clarity or ambiguity to a production, extreme symbols are impossible to ignore. At once poetic and practical, symbols can serve the action of a play and underscore meanings with visual metaphors. A striking symbol stimulates both imaginative and critical response, and when the audience goes along for the ride, symbols spark insight and revelation in ways that rational arguments can't.

Three examples. In Eugene Ionesco's *Rhinoceros*, characters transform into pachyderms when they selfishly pursue power and evade responsibility for their fellow human beings. Only the character Berenger, who experiences guilt for his past indifference, demonstrates unconditional love and thereby remains a human being at the end of the play.

In *Topdog/Underdog*, Suzan-Lori Parks creates extreme symbols in characters named Lincoln and Booth – they're brothers. She even dresses Lincoln in the classic stovepipe-hat-and-tails garb. (The character, Lincoln, reenacts President Lincoln's assassination with customers paying to shoot him with a cap gun.) Rivalry, poverty, family troubles, and betrayal lead to fratricide when Booth murders Lincoln, an inevitable tragedy that repeats its historical antecedent.

When Somebody Is Somebody is Luigi Pirandello's final play. In it, a famous author turns to stone when his adoring public won't let him innovate or deviate from the subjects and style for which he is acclaimed. Denied the opportunity to change and grow, he transforms into a living statue and takes his place alongside other adulated and deceased authors.

WORKSHOP: EXTREME SYMBOLISM

The aim of this workshop is to encourage playwrights to identify, distill, and magnify via extreme symbols the allegorical essence of their plays.

Step 1: **Write.** Playwrights write a short realistic scene with dramatic action, obstacles and conflict – or bring an existing scene to the workshop.

Step 2: **Symbolize.** Create potential extreme symbols by completing the following three sentences in reference to the scenes: 1) These characters resemble or become like _____; 2) This situation feels like _____; 3) The world of this play looks like _____.

Step 3: **Rewrite.** Apply one of these analogies to the realistic scenes, revising in order to incorporate the extreme symbol.

Step 4: **Read aloud.** If there's time, it's always interesting to read and compare the before and after scenes.

Step 5: **Discuss.** How did the symbol affect the dialogue and meanings of the play? Did it require re-thinking the characters and action? Did it make the scene more theatrical, more interesting?

◆ ◆ ◆

Borrowed Structures

We shall not cease from exploration
And the end of all our exploring
Will be to arrive where we started
And know the place for the first time.
          — T.S. Eliot, *Four Quartets/Little Gidding*

One way to break away from the linear, cause-and-effect structure of realism is to borrow structures from other disciplines and use them to organize the narrative. Here are some examples.

The title of Arthur Schnitzler's *La Ronde* refers to a circular chain dance in which all dancers hold hands or put their arms around each other's shoulders. The circular dance inspired a sequence of two-character scenes in *La Ronde*. Scene One begins with The Whore and The Soldier, proceeds to the Soldier and The Parlor Maid, and continues this way as it progresses: leaving one character behind while keeping the other on stage for the next scene with a new character. Like the dance, the partner combinations go full circle, ending with The Count and, as it began, The Whore. The structure is perfectly matched to the play's main thesis, which is that venereal diseases are transmitted via sexual liaisons that ignore boundaries of socio-economic class. Or as the concept was explained at the turn of the 21st century, when you sleep with someone, you're sleeping with everyone they've slept with, too.

A play that borrowed an architectural structure is *Sleep No More*, collaboratively written by Britain's Punchdrunk Theatre. Their American production transformed a block of empty warehouses in Manhattan into "the abandoned McKittrick Hotel." Audiences were free to wander the maze-like structure of rooms and passageways in order to forge their own journeys and interpretations of scenes staged simultaneously throughout the warehouse.

Variations on form, like those that are borrowed, also allow fascinating explorations. One standard variation is the

113

"flashback," which has been used in such plays as the Pulitzer Prize-winning *Dinner With Friends* to provide structural variety and context from the past for action in the present. Harold Pinter took the idea of the "flashback" to a logical extreme, arranging all scenes of his play *Betrayal* in reverse chronological order. As a result, the plot of *Betrayal* is rooted in effect-and-cause rather than cause-and-effect. This proved an ingenious way to de-familiarize the topic of infidelity, and by so doing offer fresh insights through moments of unexpected revelation.

WORKSHOP: BORROWED STRUCTURES

This workshop encourages playwrights to experiment with non-traditional patterns, systems, and structures for dramatic action with the aim of discovering narrative forms that might energize the theatrical experience by undermining expectations.

Step 1: **Brainstorm.** Create a list of all kinds of structures and write them on the black/whiteboard; for example, rooms in a house, sonata, limerick, abacus, alphabet, playing cards, DNA, ladder, seasons, hours in a day, weather patterns, a whodunit, jokes, swinging pendulum, a food chain.

Step 2: **Analyze.** Divide writers into groups of three or four. Ask each person to select one structure, then they will work together as a group to identify at least eight characteristics of the structures chosen by members of their group. (It's a tricky task and more minds will assist the analysis.) For example, limerick characteristics include AABBA rhyme and metric schemes, humor, surprise, sexual innuendo, often feature a woman and/or a lad, and they're Irish in origin.

Step 3: **Write.** Each playwright writes a short play incorporating as many characteristics of his or her chosen structure as possible. (Note: Writers should not simply set the play in the new structure, i.e., in each room of the house or in each of the four seasons. Encourage them to use the characteristics of those structures rather than the structures themselves. For example, consider the function of each room in the house and the qualities of each season.)

Step 4: **Read aloud.** Participants should read all the roles so the playwright (and others) can listen.

Step 5: **Discuss.** How did the characteristics of the borrowed structure inspire or color the play? How did the structure of dramatic action differ from that of a traditional linear and chronological plot? Which characteristics of the borrowed structure proved most useful in writing the play, which least, why? Did the form add to the impact of the content, did it make the play seem fresh, unique, strange, intriguing, messy, alienating?

◆ ◆ ◆

PLAYWRIGHT PERSPECTIVE:
Arthur Kopit

"Every good play takes us on a journey, and Imagination is the transport system that we use."

Why have you incorporated non-realistic theatrical elements into your plays?

First and foremost, theater is artifice. Those people up there on stage are pretending. In a certain sense, it's all a con game, and the actors' job, and the writer's and director's, is to make us in the audience believe that what they are seeing up on stage is real; not "realistic", but real. Indeed, so "real" that if one of those characters dies, and the blood we see is a long red cloth pulled out of the poor fellow's chest, we play along (because it's been so well done), and accept that he has died, and feel the loss, and (if it's been really well done) maybe even weep, and mourn.

No matter what form the play takes, even a Punch and Judy show, we have to believe in what we are seeing. It's about imagination. Stage realism is simply a convention. So what if that stove on stage is actually cooking something, and the kitchen it's in looks totally real? It's not a real kitchen, it's a stage set, and we know that, but we let it pass. We will accept it as real. That's what theatre is about.

In that sense, none of what we see on stage is "realistic", unless we define realism as just another stage convention, as fundamentally artificial as high farce. And yet, if it's done well, all of it will feel "real".

As a playwright, my job is to convince my audience that what they are seeing up there is real, and that it matters. Paradoxically, that may require using "non-realistic" elements. Say we need to get inside a character's head. How do I do that? Having the character tell us (in a soliloquy) is one way, but rarely the best. "Show don't tell" is every writer's mantra. (In musicals, characters reveal their secret thoughts in song, which is obviously non-realistic, but yet we accept it as "real".) All these are "conventions", which audiences have either come to understand, or have always understood instinctively.

So, to get inside a character's head, I have to determine what will be most effective. There's never one right answer. But whenever I have incorporated non-realistic theatrical elements in my plays, I have done so because it seemed to make what I was doing more "real", not less. It's case by case. Every good play takes us on a journey, and Imagination is the transport system that we use.

Where did (or do) you find inspiration for non-realistic elements in your plays?

When things are going well, I see what's needed instinctively. But often I do not, and when that happens, I look to my characters for the answer. That's because the very worst thing I could do at this point is just "make things up." Of course, I am making things up, but you have to be careful how you say that, because there are good ways to do it, and not so good. I won't go into the differences, it would take too much time, but they are considerable.

But let's say the stars are aligned properly, and my characters, in their own special way, tell me what to do next. When that happens, I thank them and move on. Does this constitute "inspiration"? Maybe, but I prefer to think of it as my characters simply helping out. Theatre is a collaborative medium, after all, and they need to do their share.

So that's how it works.

But sometimes it doesn't. Sometimes my characters say nothing, or, even worse, suggest something that I simply know is wrong (which I think they do just to test me).

In that case I just leave it there to sit and stew, knowing that if I've set things up properly (no easy task), the answer eventually will come.

How do you know if what you've come up with "works"? Often, that's not easy, especially if what you've come up with seems to break some major theatrical convention. Even if your gut instinct says that it does work, it may not, and you need enough humility to acknowledge at least that possibility.

The answer is, you need to hear it read, and preferably by good actors. Still, even then you may not be sure. But it does at least allow you to step back a bit. Distance is essential, and not easy to come by.

How do you make it all work, especially when you're breaking conventions?

By hearing the whole thing, and finding those places where the structure falls apart, if it does. There's a reason people who write plays are called playwrights, not play-writes. It's all about craft. Somehow, you have to find a way to make the structure work as a whole. Because it will accommodate disparate elements. But sometimes, how to do it is not readily apparent. It's empirical. Trial and error.

But always looking to your characters. We believe the world they inhabit. It's that simple. And that difficult. There's never only one right answer. But if you've done your work properly, it's in there. The solution. You just have to keep digging.

Does the opportunity to incorporate non-realistic elements in your plays allow you to explore dimensions of the human condition or tell other kinds of stories than the conventions of realism allow?

I think so. To me, strict realism is a limiting convention. Great plays are never purely one thing or another. They incorporate many elements. But if the play you're writing is primarily in a "realistic" mode, then non-realistic elements may take you off course.

But then again they may not.

You have to know why you're doing it. If what you're doing is only for effect, forget about it. Changing the modality is meant to deepen a work, not distract.

Theatre is artifice. Pretending that what's on stage is all "real" is not honest. It needs to seem real. That is all.

ARTHUR KOPIT *is the author of* Oh Dad, Poor Dad, Mamma's Hung You in the Closet and I'm Feelin' So Sad; Indians *(finalist for Pulitzer Prize);* Wings *(finalist for Pulitzer Prize);* End of the World with Symposium to Follow; *a new translation of Ibsen's* Ghosts; *the book for the musicals* Phantom *(score by Maury Yeston)*, High Society, Nine; Road to Nirvana; BecauseHeCan *(originally entitled* Y2K); Chad Curtiss, Lost Again; *and numerous one-act plays. Current projects include* Discovery of America, *a new play based on the journals of Cabeza de Vaca. Besides teaching playwriting at NYU, Mr. Kopit heads the Lark Theatre's Playwrights' Workshop and is on the Council of the Dramatists Guild.*

◆ ◆ ◆

Priority Shifts

Movies are all about plot. Theatre, even if it's story heavy, it's about ideas.
— Harvey Fierstein, Interview, *Timeoutchicago.com*

In the *Poetics*, Aristotle argued that, of the six elements of drama, plot is most important. But what happens when another of the six elements vies for theatrical prominence?

Many plays reward audiences with elements other than plot. The third scene of Caryl Churchill's *Far Away*, for example, features a parade of grey, dispirited characters modeling extravagant hats. The spectacle of the hat competition underscores the absurdity of the play's world in which only three of three hundred hats make the cut; the rest are burned with the models' bodies. With or without a plot, that spectacle drives home the theme of the play, and no description could be as vivid and disturbing as the death march hat parade.

David Hirson's comedic exploration of art and censorship, *La Bête*, is written entirely in rhymed couplets, a sort of a retro-celebration of 17th century comedy in the style of Molière. Aristotle lists diction as fourth in importance amongst the six elements, yet the witty dialogue in *La Bête* is definitely a main attraction.

In William McNulty's recently published adaptation of Balderstam and Dean's original stage version of *Dracula,* there are fangs, blood, and stakes pounded through hearts. That's what audiences love about that annual production at Actors Theatre of Louisville. Though Aristotle considered spectacle the least important of the six dramatic elements, scary spectacle is the audience's priority in that production.

The idea that plays might be driven by spectacle, music, ideas, or language rather than plot and character, raises the question: What is a play? Aristotle defines a kind of play, but hardly the only kind. In many parts of the world, the idea of a play is synonymous with a theatrical event that actors perform in a space over time for an audience. Insisting on the defining elements prescribed in

Poetics deprives the theatre of imaginative potential and limits the types of experiences that playwrights and performers might create for audiences – and why would anyone want to do that?

Workshop: Priority Shifts

As with most of the workshops in this book, priority shifts require novel ways of thinking about plays as well as writing them. This workshop is designed to alter the audience experience through a non-traditional emphasis on dramatic elements. The workshop will hopefully raise questions about paradigms of dramatic structure, definitions of plot and theatrical event, and perhaps even the social and aesthetic purposes of theatre itself.

Step 1: **Write.** Begin by writing a short realistic scene with action, obstacles, and conflict; in other words, a conventional scene. Or bring an existing scene to the workshop.

Step 2: **Brainstorm.** As a group, write all the dramatic and theatrical elements the group can think of on the white/ blackboard (costumes, music, lights, scale, sound, color, character, argument, confession, accusation, climax, props, dance, blackouts, etc.).

Step 3: **Select.** Thinking of the scenes each playwright wrote or brought, which topic on the list offers the most potential in terms of prioritizing that aspect of the scene? For example, could a revised scene be further theatricalized by emphasizing color or sound?

Step 4: **Imagine.** Writers consider ways their chosen theatrical element can dominate their scenes.

Step 5: **Revise.** Playwrights rewrite their scenes emphasizing the element they've chosen. Ideally, the element should be so important that it becomes a "character" in the scene. Other characters must acknowledge, respond to, and interact with it. As with any character, it should

121

have an arc in the scene: does it take over or disappear, proliferate or disintegrate, disturb or comfort, determine or challenge?

Step 6: **Read aloud.** Participants should read all the roles so the playwright (and others) can listen.

Step 7: **Discuss.** How has expanding the presence or increasing the significance of one theatrical element affected the experience of listening to the play? Are the human characters diminished in importance or further defined? Does the scene hold more or less interest – is it more or less energetic, surprising, mysterious?

Step 8: **Begin again.** This time, writers start with a theatrical element and build a play around it. Is it possible to write a play in which light or sound, an object or activity, outweighs the importance of plot or character development and yet delivers a satisfying experience for an audience?

◆ ◆ ◆

The Mystical, Supernatural and Paranormal

Mystical: *having a spiritual meaning or reality that is neither apparent to the senses nor obvious to the intelligence.*
Supernatural: *of or relating to an order of existence beyond the visible observable universe.*
Paranormal: *not scientifically explainable.*
— *Merriam-Webster Dictionary*

One aspect of theatre common to all cultures around the world is the representation of gods, spirits, demons, and supernatural figures whose interventions on behalf of or in opposition to human aspirations emphasize the spiritual dimensions of life on earth. Monkey gods, Olympians and Titans, Thunderbird and Coyote, Ogun, Beelzebub – all these deities and more provided the narratives for ancient dramas, which were full of magic and myth. But not so much anymore on stage.

There are always exceptions, of course, and quite notable ones, including the Troll King in Ibsen's *Peer Gynt*, the formless fears and crocodile god in O'Neill's *The Emperor Jones*, and Mr. Applegate (the Devil) in the musical *Damn Yankees*. In contemporary drama, supernatural characters are most likely to appear as a ghost or memory of a relative or friend, as they do in *Da, Proof,* and *Blithe Spirit*. Occasionally, however, celestial and mythological figures do appear – the Guardian Angel in José Rivera's *Marisol*, title character in Carson Kreitzer's *Lilith,* and the zombie apocalypse in Jackie Sibblies Drury's *Social Creatures*.

Mixing the imaginary and the "real" can create narratives that are unusual and, for that reason alone, intriguing. Also, to justify the presence of supernatural characters, playwrights tend to grant them strong passions and clear purposes, which clarifies dramatic action and sharpens conflict. "Let the great work begin!" declares the Angel, announcing the timeliness and significance of her arrival at the end of Tony Kushner's *Angels in America: Millennium Approaches*.

Recent works by two of the playwrights interviewed in this volume illustrate how supernatural characters and elements can make the plays more exciting for themselves and others. The dramaturgical advantages of incorporating supernatural characters into otherwise realistic plays are evident in Naomi Wallace's *Liquid Plain*, which is excerpted below. This poetic historical drama features Bristol, a 40-year-old African-American woman, who encounters a dead body "come to life" on the shipping docks of 19th century Rhode Island. Bristol's conversation, however, is not with the person who inhabited that body in life. That's the great thing about the realm of the supernatural – you get to make up your own rules.

(...Then the body opens its cage and steps out.)

BRISTOL: Do I know you?

BODY: My name is William. You've got my book in your pocket.

(Bristol checks to see that the book is still in her pocket. She's relieved.)

BODY: Though sadly only the verse. Have you seen the engravings?

BRISTOL: Yes. At the bookshop.

BODY: I miss the painting far more than the words. The right colors can give you a blow to your chest, a deadly blow, much like love. Words are merely what come after love, to placate the emptiness. *(Beat)* I never was happy with that last line either. Irony is a cheap ejaculation. I prefer its whorish neighbors: polemic, expostulation, mockery, hyperbole, provocation, abuse, which polite society so often misreads in my verse. I'll change that line. What would you prefer I say?

BRISTOL: William Blake died in England in 1827. I cannot be speaking to you.

BLAKE/BODY: Why not? I conversed with my dead brother Robert all my life.

BRISTOL: In a gibbetting cage?

BLAKE: No. In my head. But it's a similar machine.

BRISTOL: I'm lost. You frighten me. And you have a terrible smell.

BLAKE: I won't apologize as this isn't my body. It's rare that I land in a rotter like this. Not pleasant at all. But when someone, in this instance you, recites my verse near the dying, for a brief few moments I'm here again, inside their expiring flesh. Dying or dead is the only harbor I can reach now. That's my deal with the Almighty for having penned him a few rather fine verses in my time...

In barely a minute's dialogue, this encounter generates mystery, discovery, wonder, literary allusion, conflict, and sensory overload. It would be difficult to accomplish as much in such a brief passage with a realistic drama. Furthermore, by introducing one supernatural phenomenon, Wallace opens the doors to more, in this case, a gigantic parasite.

> *(Suddenly there is a tremendous splash, as though something has just hurled itself into the water. Dembi, Gifford and Nesbitt are startled. Then we hear a swimming noise; a giant five-foot Guinea worm has surfaced. They all look into the water. We do not see the worm, but they do. Dembi steps back and the sailors cry out in fear.)*

DEMBI: That be the biggest damn Guinea worm I ever seen.

The Guinea worm assists Bristol in her search for justice, finding its way somehow to the house of James De Woolf, a former U. S. Senator who murdered Bristol's aunt by throwing her overboard mid-way through a trans-Atlantic voyage.

> *(De Wolf stands alone, again regarding the painting. There is a soft knocking. He think's it's the door. At first he doesn't respond. Then the knocking comes again, a little stronger.)*

DE WOOLF: Come in. *(Beat)* Who's there? *(Beat)* Who's there?

(De Woolf imagines he's just hearing things. He sits in his chair, still, thinking. Behind him, a small hole appears in the center of the painting. Then it gets larger. The painting quietly tears open to allow the hint of a thick shadow, of a 'darkness,' to appear in the hole. We do not see the worm, only a possible shadow. De Woolf does not see it. We hear the sound of something sliding through the painting into the room. Then the shadow vanishes in the dark, as though it had never been. After a moment, De Woolf itches himself. He feels a stronger itch elsewhere and itches it. Then he's motionless again. Lights out on De Woolf.)

By adding supernatural elements to her historical setting, Wallace reminds viewers that the play is not "real," and any audience member willing to suspend its disbelief receives the pleasures of complicity in Wallace's acts of poetic imagination.

It's also possible to flip the equation. Rather than introducing supernatural figures into a realistic world, it's possible to take regular humans to mythic and fictional lands, because a place that never or no longer exists is a space where anything can happen. Think Dorothy in *The Wizard of Oz* or Mr. Zero, who travels to the Elysian Fields following his trial and execution in Elmer Rice's *The Adding Machine*. Once in heaven, Mr. Zero discovers Hope in the form of a female character who may or may not exist.

In Arthur Kopit's *Discovery of America*, characters in view of the audience are seen by some but not others onstage; they exist simultaneously in the 16th and 21st centuries; they inhabit Spain, Florida, Texas, and Mexico City all at once; and they're transported through time and space in ways that none can explain. The paranormal, supernatural, and mystical intermingle in a journey through dimensions that would baffle even Einstein. What makes this potentially incomprehensible jumble of time and space compelling and comprehensible is that Kopit embraces the paradox, acknowledges the impossibility, and revels in the absurdity of it all. And as his characters come to terms with the irrationality of their universe – they have to, because within the play the consequences of their actions are real – so do we. In the following excerpt, The Adviser functions as a surrogate for the audience who also need to buy into the curious logic of the play.

> *(Lights back up on the Adviser's Office, where a great carousing is now going on between the Adviser, the Candidate, and Ernesto, who is serving as bartender, mixing drinks from the Maguey plant. In the background, the three Conquistadors still look on.)*

THE ADVISER: This is really not bad!

THE CANDIDATE: Have some more.

THE ADVISER: Don't mind if I do. By the way, what's in this drink? It tastes a bit different from before.

ERNESTO: Oh, just a bit of this, a bit of that.

> *(Ernesto pours him one more. The Advisor downs it. Something about that one seems to do the trick. Suddenly he sees the three Conquistadors!)*

THE ADVISER: *Oh my God!*

DORANTES: Andres Dorantes … *(with a flourish)* ¡Á vestro servicio!

CASTILLO: Alonso del Castillo… *(similar flourish)* ¡Á vestro servicio!

ESTABAN: Estebanico… *(grandest flourish of all)* ¡Á vestro servicio!

THE ADVISER: … What happened to …

DORANTES: Cabeza de Vaca?

> *(The Adviser nods.)*

CASTILLO: We have come to take you to him.

DORANTES: He's not been well.

THE CANDIDATE: They think maybe we can help.

THE ADVISER: … *We?*

ERNESTO: Yes.

THE ADVISER: No, I'm sorry. This is not possible.

DORANTES: That's what people said when they first heard about *us*.

ESTEBAN: What have you got to lose?

THE ADVISER: I don't know.

ERNESTO: *Only one way to find out!*

THE ADVISER: No, I'm sorry. *No!*

THE CANDIDATE: You want to find out which way they went? *This is how to do it.*

THE ADVISER: I thought you didn't care which way they went.

THE CANDIDATE: I don't. But it obviously matters to you, and I want you with me.

THE ADVISER: *Oh God...*

ERNESTO: *(to the Candidate)* If he doesn't want to come, leave him. *They are satisfied with just you.*

THE ADVISER: No, no! I will come. What historian could say no to a chance like this? *(to his nephew)* You do realize though...

THE CANDIDATE: It's unorthodox, no, I understand.

THE ADVISER: Well, just so long as you do... *(to the conquistadors)* Lead on, Macduff!

(A SHIP begins to form around them!)

THE ADVISOR: *Oh Jesus....*

(SOUND of raging wind, waves, a mast cracking.)

THE CANDIDATE: Hang on to me and you'll be fine.

VARIOUS VOICES: Look fast! / Watch it! / Quick! The rigging! / Furl the sails! / Here comes another one! / To the rigging! Quick! *(etc.)*

(One of those struggling to control the ship has a red beard and a patch over one eye. His name is Pánfilo de Narváez and he's in command – or, at least, is supposed to be.)

NARVÁEZ: Starboard! I said to starboard! Starboard! Starboard! *(etc.)*

THE ADVISER: Who's that?

THE CANDIDATE: Narváez.

ERNESTO: Stay clear of him and you'll be all right.

(Narváez spots The Adviser.)

NARVÁEZ: What's *he* doing up here?

DORANTES: He's with us.

NARVÁEZ: Well put him to work! STARBOARD! I SAID TO STARBOARD! DID NOBODY HEAR ME?

DORANTES: We all did, sire, but the wind countermanded your instructions.

SAILOR # 2: Below! Hold fast! The topsail's gone!

FRIAR SOLIS: Here, sire. A bible. Use it.

(Friar Solis hands Narváez a bible.)

NARVÁEZ: Don't understand it... *All our efforts...*

THE ADVISER: But where is Cabeza deVaca?

DORANTES: Out there... *somewhere...*

THE ADVISER: But I thought he was on this ship, too.

CASTILLO: He is.

THE ADVISER: ... But ...

DORANTES: He is in *both* places.

CASTILLO: We are in the realm of memory now.

DORANTES: We are all in *many* places now.

CASTILLO: *(sotto voce)* He does not like Narváez, and only comes aboard when absolutely necessary.

ERNESTO: Don't worry. They have taken this journey many times.

DORANTES: Ah! There he is!

(A faint light illumines Cabeza deVaca, far away, faint hint of the cell bars around him.)

THE ADVISER: He looks to be in a jail.

CASTILLO: And so he is.

DORANTES: But with us as well.

CASTILLO: I know; it makes no sense.

DORANTES: After awhile, one gets used to it.

CABEZA deVACA: *(calling from the distance)* Are you not ready for me yet?

DORANTES: Not quite, m'lord! Worry not! We'll call you when we are!

CASTILLO: Yes... *What to make of it...*

(And then, all at once, the storm grows worse.)

ONE OF THE SAILORS: Hold fast! THE NEXT WAVE SINKS US ALL!

> *(The Adviser and his nephew grab a rope and cling to it for dear life. As they do...)*

THE ADVISER: I'm curious; when you invited me aboard, were you aware that this was about to happen?

Drug trip, memory, time travel, portals, purgatory... Yes, what to make of it, indeed. "Every good play takes us on a journey," explains Kopit in his *Perspective*, "and Imagination is the transport system that we use."

Workshop #1: The Mystical, Supernatural, and Paranormal

These two workshops encourage playwrights to utilize their powers of imagination rather than observation by enriching their plays – narratively, dramaturgically, and thematically – with aspects of myth, fantasy, fairy tales, and inexplicable phenomena.

Step 1: **Research**. Writers identify and research gods, demigods, devils, angels, demons, fairies, folkloric and/or mythical characters who have been forgotten, neglected, or, at the very least, aren't well known. What are their traits, their *raison d'être*, their inconsistencies and quirks, their relationships to humans and other fantastical figures? How do they fit into the pecking order of their cosmologies?

Step 2: **Select**. Writers choose one of these characters to insert in an otherwise realistic situation.

Step 3: **Write**. Playwrights write a short play in which the fantasy characters become involved in the dramatic action. Their purpose should be clear, though their appearance should add confusion, complications, and conflict. (No *deus ex machina*, please. It's preferable to have gods or fairies cause problems rather than solve them.) How does their arrival change the rules of the play? How do they affect the laws of physics? What are their powers and how do they use them? Something unexplainable or impossible should happen. These characters also bring with them an idea, a reason they exist in the first place, and their essential purpose should be central to the human problems in the play. A perfect example is Terrence McNally's *A Perfect Ganesh*, in which the Hindu god Ganesha aids two troubled women on their spiritual quests for peace and acceptance during their remarkable journey through India.

Step 4: **Read**. Participants should read the roles so that the playwright (and others) can listen.

Step 5: **Discuss**. What did the fantastic characters contribute to the play, and how interesting would the plays have been without them? What themes or ideas did the imagined characters introduce, skew, or complicate? Did they have an action, and were they changed in the course of events?

WORKSHOP #2: THE MYSTICAL, SUPERNATURAL, AND PARANORMAL

Step 1: **Brainstorm.** As a group, brainstorm a list of non-realistic settings for a play. Include fictional lands like Oz and Jurassic Park, mythological sites like Mount Olympus and Valhalla, psychological ideas such as memory or hallucinations, geographical zones like the bottom of the sea or inside a volcano, distant planets and faraway galaxies, and mystical concepts like "the other side" or spirit world.

Step 2: **Research and report.** Writers select several locations and research facts and descriptions, images and histories. Present the findings – inventions, dreams, and fantasies of the past can liberate a writer's imagination.

131

Step 3: **Select and write.** Playwrights write a short play set in one of the locations. The setting should affect the play's dramatic action and contribute to its meanings through metaphor, cosmology, or allusion.

Step 4: **Read.** Participants read all the roles so the playwright (and others) can listen.

Step 5: **Discuss.** How important is setting or location to creating atmosphere and shaping action? How do ideas implicit in the location inform the meanings of the play? Do the stage directions or descriptions differ in style or substance from those in realistic plays? Was the experience of the audience different from listening to a realistic play?

◆◆◆

PLAYWRIGHT PERSPECTIVE:
Naomi Wallace

"I welcome the dead into my work, and time travellers ..."

Why have you incorporated non-realistic theatrical elements into your plays?

How to put flesh and bone onto those who are dead, that is what challenges me. Only on the stage can the dead come to life again in such an intimate and tactile manner. History is carried in our bodies and to be inside the past, we have to travel through time, without the baggage of restrictive notions of the possible. I welcome the dead into my work, and time travellers (such as Cod in *Slaughter City*). Often the dead are more interesting than the living, and surprising. And yet I try and be careful not to use ghosts as a mere trick, or as filler for the empty lives of the living. If I do, the ghosts will not co-operate and end up kicking me in the ass and exiting without warning.

Where do you find inspiration for non-realistic elements in your plays?

For my new play, *The Liquid Plain*, I read, among many other books, Marcus Rediker's brilliant *The Slave Ship*. In it he recounts the story of an 18th century Black woman captive who was thrown overboard a ship called *The Polly*. The details around this story haunt me. It is a kind of violation to take on the voice of those who are dead but I see it as a listening rather than a "taking". When I read history, its ghosts inspire me. The past is not quiet but full of noise, raucous love, and calling, as well as violence and resistance.

Does the opportunity to incorporate non-realistic elements in your plays allow you to explore dimensions of the human condition or tell other kinds of stories than the conventions of realism allow?

Realism (as well as "the human condition") is a construct as much as any other. The mistake we may make is to believe in

133

an agreed upon notion of "reality" and to assume that when we stray from it, we are opting for the "unreal." Realism on stage, in general, is what is acceptable (and material) to the status quo. What lurks and calls on the periphery is more difficult for mainstream ideology to co-opt. The past, the dead, the unseen are as real or unreal as any other moment of our experience.

NAOMI WALLACE *is a playwright and poet whose awards include an Obie, the Susan Smith Blackburn Prize, the Kesselring Prize, and a MacArthur Fellowship, popularly known as the genius award. Her plays have been produced around the world, including* The Inland Sea *(The Oxford Stage Company and the Oregon Shakespeare Festival) and* One Flea Spare *(The Bush Theatre, Actors Theatre of Louisville and the Comédie Francaise).* Slaughter City *premiered at the Royal Shakespeare Company and* The Trestle at Pope Lick Creek *premiered in the Humana Festival of New American Plays and was later produced at the Edinburgh Theatre. She's written screenplays for the films* Lawn Dogs *and* The War Boys.

◆ ◆ ◆

Interruptions

Control is the enemy of art.
 – Robert Rauschenberg, *Rauschenberg/Art and Life*

Evan Bergman, a friend and talented actor, tells a story about a production of *Glengarry Glen Ross* in which he'd been cast. Rehearsals went well and the opening night performance was clipping along to the staccato beat of David Mamet's dialogue. Then the restaurant walls fell on the actors, who somehow managed to stop them from falling on the audience. And that's what everyone remembers, because a real event on stage required a real response – there was no "ism" involved.

When events, planned or otherwise, interrupt an audience's vicarious involvement with characters on stage, the illusion of reality is displaced by an awareness of both life and artifice. Brecht created his theories of Epic Theatre and methods of alienation to arouse this type of critical consciousness in the audience. But there are other ways to jar audiences from their willing suspension of disbelief, and here are four of them.

Authenticity

Julie Marie Myatt traveled to Cambodia twice to research sex trafficking with minors so that she could write *Boats on a River*, which premiered at the Guthrie Theater. Since the subject matter was inappropriate as theatrical entertainment for young girls who were the ages of the characters – 5, 7, 13 – Myatt suggested casting adult women instead. The audience accepted the convention … until the end. That's when two adult actors were replaced on stage by girls ages 5 and 7, and that's when the audience gasped. Clearly, the children themselves were still "actors," but the reality of their age and size was shocking because the stage convention of adults playing children, which protected the audience from visceral discomforts of the topic, had vanished. Myatt's *coup de téâtre* did not undermine the preceding two hours' traffic of the stage; rather, it moved the audience from the safety of the *idea* of sex trafficking with minors in an abstracted setting into a group of adults sharing the space with actual children who were the ages of the victims themselves. It was a show-stopping moment in the best sense of the term.

Another example is Jon Lipsky's *The Survivor: A Cambodian Odyssey*, which depicts Dr. Haing S. Ngor's performance as Dith Pran in *The Killing Fields*, for which he won the Academy Award for Best Supporting Actor in 1985. The play relates Ngor's own story of torture by the Khmer Rouge which he re-experiences as he plays the role of Dith Pran. Lipsky's play follows this double helix structure of a character playing a character in two stories of survival. At play's end, however, Lipsky and director Vinnie Murphy broke the illusion of their realistic production when a member of the Cambodian Royal Ballet Company entered from backstage and sang a song from her nation's classical repertoire. Again, the "ism" on the real fell away as the audience discovered themselves in the presence of an artist who had herself been targeted by the Khmer Rouge and escaped the Killing Fields. It was a stunning meta-theatrical moment.

When presenting a version of reality on stage, there is a significant difference between "ism" and "it". This explains why a talentless Toto can upstage a talented Dorothy – all it takes is a well-timed doggie yawn, scratch, or lick to destroy the illusion of Oz.

WORKSHOP: AUTHENTICITY

Step 1: **Research**. Writers research groups and individuals – all living – who interest them. The possibilities are endless, but here are a few examples where interviews led to plays: the Delaney sisters (*Having Our Say* by Emily Mann), female Vietnam veterans (Shirley Lauro's *A Piece of My Heart*), and homeless citizens living in Louisville (*Whereabouts Unknown* by Barbara Damashek). In none of those works, however, did actual subjects of the drama appear in the play.

Step 2: **Discuss and analyze.** Why have the writers been drawn to their subjects? What do they consider their dramatic or theatrical potential? How would they incorporate someone from that group into a script and production? How might the appearance of the actual person or persons break through the conventions of realism – and once the conventions are broken, what then?

Step 3: **Write.** When the writers have found ways to incorporate their person or persons into the theatrical production, they should proceed to write a short play.

Step 4: **Read.** Other writers, or actors if they are available, read all the parts so the playwright can listen. If the actual person who's incorporated into the play is available, is it a good idea to invite them to hear the reading – or ask them to read their "role"? If so, do it.

Step 5: **Discuss.** How would the appearance of an actual person involved in the story (rather than that person being represented as a character) have altered the experience for the audience? Did it add, distract, make the audience self-conscious, or leave the audience wondering more about the person than the play? Would the audience ask more questions of the performance, and would those questions, suspicions, doubts, or amazement contribute to the value of the theatrical experience?

◆ ◆ ◆

CHOICE

In Alan Ayckbourn's play *Intimate Exchanges*, the actors are given a choice to make at the end of each scene, and each choice leads to its own next scene. This pattern repeats itself four times until each night's audience sees only 5 of the 31 possible scenes and finishes with just one of the sixteen endings. Jeffrey Jones's *70 Scenes from Halloween* calls for someone/anyone to select and say scene numbers aloud during the performance so the actors can perform that scene next. The Neo-Futurists in Chicago ask the audience to select 30 plays in any order, but quickly, so that the actors can perform all 30 plays in 60 minutes.

Plot choices are offered to audiences viewing the musical *The Mystery of Edwin Drood*. Since Dickens never finished this book, composer/lyricist/librettist Rupert Holmes decided to let the audience vote on the ending. The audience is asked to vote on a replacement for the lead actor/character (the character leaves the production in a huff, as scripted), identify the murderer, and select any two characters to fall in love. Their choices require cast members to change roles and costumes and be ready to sing all the songs in all the endings that Rupert wrote to make this scheme work out.

The act of choosing reminds an audience that actors are performers as well as characters. Raising audience awareness of choices or putting them in control of the narrative sequence removes the invisible Fourth Wall that separates actors from audience. By shouting out scene numbers, everyone gets in on the act; the audience develops a rooting interest in the event and a more personal relationship with the performers. In the examples above, realism is replaced by participatory theatricality that highlights the pleasures of collaborative choice.

WORKSHOP: CHOICE

Choice is the turning point of dramatic action. It is the end product of a thought process, and thought process, or subtext, according to Stanislavski, is what spectators come to the theatre to hear. But what happens when audiences participate with characters in their thought processes or, conversely, what happens when audiences are empowered to make choices for the characters? This workshop challenges writers to demolish the Fourth Wall (and possibly the First, Second, and Third walls, as well) by involving the audience in choices that characters make to forward the plot.

Step 1: **Plan.** Writers outline a scene or scenes that require characters to make a series of choices along the way.

Step 2: **Decide**. Writers then decide how to involve an out-sider in those choices. "Outsiders" can include one or more members of the audience, director, playwright, or someone not even present in the theatre (perhaps they're available by phone, text, email).

Step 3: **Write**. Playwrights write a scene or scenes in which an "outsider" helps a character make a choice. What do outsiders need to know in order to make a suggestion or the choice itself? What does the character need the outsiders to know before making the choice? Does the act of choosing become a scene unto itself?

Step 4: **Read**. Workshop participants read the script and fill in as "outsiders" so the playwright can observe.

Step 5: **Discuss**. What happened when the character was not in control of her or his destiny? Who is in the spotlight – the outsider/decision-maker or the character – and what are the stakes for each? Does a relationship develop be-tween actor/character and outsider/decision-maker, and how does outsider involvement affect audience percep-tion of the characters and the overall event?

◆ ◆ ◆

CHANCE

Like it or not, chance plays a huge role in our lives, though not so much in our art. Given the high price of tickets charged by major theatres, most audience members want a guaranteed experience. Few are willing to "take a chance" at the box of-fice, which explains the programming at many large theatres: recognizable titles, popular authors, recent New York hits. The need for financial security in our society is matched by a need for entertainment dependability.

The problem with guaranteed anything is that chance adds significant spice to life. Known quantities are, well, known. They may live up to expectations or not, but they generally don't offer much surprise. Also, if people weren't attracted to chance, there'd be no Publisher's Clearinghouse, no Las Vegas, no Friday nights hanging out at the bar waiting to hook up.

According to the *Merriam-Webster Dictionary*, chance is "something that happens unpredictably without discernible human intention or observable cause." How does one do that in the arts? In the visual arts, Marcel Duchamp used chance as an artistic process in the making of *3 Standard Stoppages*, as he dropped three strings onto cloth and encased their random curves in glass plates. That work along with its accompanying notes and boxes has become a landmark of modern art.

How do we capitalize on chance in the theatre? It's not like Hamlet decides what to do by flipping a coin. And rehearsals are all about getting intentions right and actions defined and repeatable. But *what if* the outcome of the drama was determined by a role of the dice? Or a fierce competition of musical chairs, as it is in Janet Allard's *Vrooommm!*, in which five NASCAR drivers vie for supremacy in an all-out, no-holds-barred, metaphorical musical car race to see who gets to sit in the champion driver's seat when the music cuts out?

When the outcome is uncertain or varies from night to night, "live" theatre resembles life in ways that plays with charted journeys and predetermined endings can't. How can playwrights tap the excitement of uncertainty in the carefully constructed universe of written and rehearsed plays? One way is for playwrights to script chance into the theatrical event.

WORKSHOP: CHANCE

The element of chance is most dramatic when the stakes are high, when there's a million bucks riding on the spin of a roulette wheel or Super Bowl teams await the coin toss to see which team receives the ball first in overtime. This workshop challenges playwrights to insert the element of chance – and then deal with all possible consequences – at a pivotal moment in their plays.

Step 1: **Brainstorm.** In what ways does chance play a role in our lives? (Games, gambling, timing, encounters, DNA, etc.)

Step 2: **Discuss.** What are the mechanisms of chance that a playwright might use to determine the outcome of the play (dice, Tarot cards, Chinese fortune sticks, Russian roulette, coin toss, children's counting games like "She loves me, she loves me not," paper-rock-scissors)?

Step 3: **Write.** Playwrights write a short play incorporating a chance outcome at an important moment. Make sure the stakes are high so that the outcome of the chance event is crucial to the dramatic action and audience's rooting interest.

Step 4: **Read.** Workshop participants read the script so the playwright can listen. Are non-readers/audience members involved in the moment of chance?

Step 5: **Analyze.** How did the element of chance affect the play? Did chance increase or diminish audience interest? Would this work best with large or small audiences, big or intimate spaces? Are the paths not taken – the endings left out by chance – of interest to audiences, as well? Are there ways theatre can incorporate chance that are different from game or reality shows on television?

◆◆◆

ACCIDENTS

Preview performances for *Spiderman: Turn Off the Dark* on Broadway offered a stark lesson in morbid curiosity. Despite reviews that should have kept audiences away in droves ("ungodly, indecipherable mess" – *New York Times*), the record number of

183 previews drew full houses. The main attraction? Interruptions due to technical difficulties and actor injuries. This one-of-a-kind production quickly garnered an appealing reputation as one-of-a-dangerous-kind.

Another slightly less gruesome tale of theatrical accidents was reported on the radio program *This American Life* in an episode titled "Fiasco!". (Check it out at www.thisamericanlife.org/radio-archives/espisode/61/fiasco.) As recounted by someone who attended that notorious production of *Peter Pan*, Hook's hook flew off the actor's hand and hit an old woman in the stomach, the fire alarm brought firemen to clear the house, and actors (members of Tiger Lily's tribe) fell from the balcony into the audience and were whisked away by the EMS. Years later, locals in that town still marvel at that ill-fated production. Had everything gone according to plan and as rehearsed, would the production have made such a lasting impression? No way.

Accidents pose a special challenge for playwrights: How to harness the theatrical dynamite that's inherent in spills and mishaps without sending actors to the hospital. If you plan for the possibility, of course, it's less an accident than a matter of chance. One possibility is to write a play in which misfortune plays a significant part. Writing, rehearsing, and staging a scene that's interrupted by an "accident" can be as compelling for an audience as watching an actual accident – and much safer for everyone involved in the production.

There are the mental accidents, as well. These Freudian slips, otherwise known as parapraxis, include slips of the pen, misreadings, mishearings, and temporary memory loss. The fun of Mark O'Donnell's ten-minute play, *Marred Bliss*, is sparked entirely by the sexual innuendo of his characters' slips of the tongue, as evidenced in this excerpt.

JANE: Oh honey, just *sink!*
DINK: What do you want me to sink about?
JANE: In less than forty-eight horrors, you and I will be moan and woof! *(grins)* Isn't it amassing?
DINK: It *is* amassing. *(lowers his paper thoughtfully)* So much has harpooned in just a few thief years!

JANE: It steams like only yesterday that you were the noise next door.

DINK: And you were that feckless-faced cod sitting up in the old ache tree!

JANE: And now we're encaged! I can hardly wait till we're marred!

DINK: Oh, Hiney! *(makes to enfold her in his arms)*

JANE: Now, now! I'm sure the tame will pass quickly till our hiney-moon! (eases out of his grasp) I'll go get you some of that nice saltpeter taffy that Smother brought back from A Frantic City.

Accidents that occur in the process of writing can also be worth keeping, as reported in this instance by playwright/performer Kevin Kling, who uses a voice-activated program to write his performance monologues. His computer registered his dachshund's barking as "How? How?" Believe it or not, the computer also recorded his cat's meow as "Why?" Kevin incorporated both these computer error/Zen animal questions in his book, *The Dog Says How.*

Workshop: Accidents

Accidents change our perception time, hence the phrase, "It's like watching a car crash in slow motion." Scientists have documented the phenomenon of time slowing down for people involved in an accident even though it occurs at normal speed. The goal of this workshop is for writers to elicit the hilarity and/or horror of accidents in a scripted play through the manipulation of time or slips of the mind and tongue.

Step 1: **Share**. Workshop participants recount accidents they've seen or experienced, noting whether time slowed down for the people involved.

Step 2: **Analyze**. What makes those stories memorable or interesting, amusing or sorrowful, horrific or redeeming? Did a changing perception of time or an awareness of mental flaws contribute to the fascination of the story?

143

Step 3: **Discuss.** How can the sudden, unexpected, and unfortunate aspects of accidents interrupt dramatic action? Is that similar or different to ways that accidents impact or interrupt people's lives?

Step 4: **Write**. Playwrights write a scene that's interrupted by a scripted accident and then deals with the aftermath. Playwrights should experiment with changing perceptions of time and mental mishaps, as well.

Step 5: **Read.** Writers bring copies of their plays so that others can read the roles while the playwright listens.

Step 6: **Discuss.** Which side of the accident – before or after – was more interesting? Why? What did the manipulation of time passing contribute that would not have been possible in normal time? Did the mental mishaps reveal something about the character that would otherwise have been difficult or impossible to convey?

◆ ◆ ◆

Rebellion

The only way to deal with an unfree world is to become so absolutely free that your very existence is an act of rebellion.
  – Albert Camus, *The Rebel: an Essay on Man in Revolt*

In the movie *Network*, a news anchor implores his television audience to open their windows and shout: "I'm as mad as hell, and I'm not going to take this anymore!" And they do. His passionate battle cry unleashes a pent-up national fury.

In plays that audiences perceive as powerful, characters are almost always driven by anger or fear. Consider these: *Oedipus, Othello, Romeo and Juliet, A Doll's House, The Normal Heart, How I Learned To Drive, Little Foxes, Keely and Du*. In each, a character's anger or fear distorts relationships and leads to catastrophic events.

For characters, rage and dread overpower compassion. A character's anger is self-centered, judgmental, and vengeful, and fear inspires a fight-or-flight response. Those passions are crucial to great drama because they demand action, usually rebellion against an oppressive status quo.

A case in point is *The Normal Heart*. While Larry Kramer's political activism is well served by realism on stage, it is ultimately the playwright's unapologetic rage that accounts for the play's enduring power. Commenting on his 2012 revival of the play, California Shakespeare director Jon Moscone noted, "Larry is right on target; the anger has kept his writing – this play in particular – on fire, a pulsing and undeniable *cri de coeur*."

It was fear for the future of her children that motivated JoAnne Akalaitis to create *Dead End Kids: A History of Nuclear Power*. That Mabou Mines production, conceived and directed by Akalaitis, took the form of a polemic composed of comedy, science, alchemy, myth, history, and explosions. The ability to tap the fears of its audience accounted for the play's profound impact, according to *Village Voice* critic Erika Munk, who wrote this about the 1980 production at the Public Theater:

145

A brave, astonishing event.

What's brave is that it takes on our worst fears about the future—the ones barely faced in private, rarely in art, abstractly in social science, never in theatre. And what's astonishing is that Mabou Mines—a group praised and damned for many things, but never yet for its politics—has merged uncompromising experimental theatricality with outfront didactic intent.

It's about time. Theatre no longer addresses our inner lives with any intensity, and ignores that outside world which, finally, controls us.

["'Dead End Kids': Signaling Through the Flames," *VV*, Nov. 12, 1980]

Great passion need not break from conventions of realism to be effective on stage, but a playwright's intense anger or fear can instigate a break from realism when staging conventions prove restrictive and trite. And, further to Munk's point, perhaps the best way to express our inner lives with intensity is to find new theatrical forms in which to portray them.

So what makes you mad? What injustice infuriates you? What's going on in "that outside world," as Munk termed it, that you outright reject? What vision of the future do you fear? Can you express your deepest feelings and wildest thoughts within the familiar situations and recognizable encounters of a realistic play? If not, what needs to change, what needs to go?

WORKSHOP #1: REBELLION (PASSIONS, NOT RULES)

This workshop encourages writers to break realistic conventions by following feelings of anger and fear without concern for tradition or form.

Step 1: **Select.** Each playwright selects a text that prompts in them a strong negative reaction (anger or fear). They bring a copy to class, and for the purposes of the workshop, any genre will do. If the playwright hopes the work will lead to publication or production, it's best to select a text that's in the public domain (generally anything published before 1920).

Step 2: **Summarize.** Playwrights summarize the content of the text in a paragraph or brief presentation. This step helps writers focus on those elements of the text that provoke the strongest reaction.

Step 3: **Pre-writing.** Writers examine their reactions to the text, and describe how it feels, what it provokes in them, do they have any physiological responses. They do not have to share this list with anyone.

Step 4: **Write.** Each playwright writes a scene – a theatrical event in which the original text is spoken in an extreme dramatic context that conveys the playwright's feelings. Playwrights can excerpt whatever they like from the original text, and they can add any other text, images, characters, events that express their feelings. There are no rules or limits, let passion be your guide. For example, if the ideas in the text make the writer fear for the future, the playwright can create an image or event in which a character is threatened by water, war, oppression, etc. The point is for the writers to put their emotions into an image that creates a dramatic event when combined with the text.

Step 5: **Read.** Pass out copies of the scripts so that partici-pants can read all the parts while the playwright (and others) listen.

Step 6: **Discuss.** What feelings did the event provoke in the listeners? How did the text and image/event interrelate: as a dialectic, a confrontation, an ironic juxtaposition? How did the contrast of spoken text with image/event change the meaning of the original text?

WORKSHOP #2: REBELLION (NEW ENDINGS FOR A NEW ERA)

This workshop encourages writers to question authority, subvert tradition, and challenge classical ideas by revising them to their own satisfaction. It gives writers permission to play around with the past, to engage in a dialogue with dead authors, and to use classic texts to explore contemporary concerns. The goal is to create a dialectical tension between classical and contemporary worldviews. Playwrights will succeed to the degree they gain confidence in their abilities to engage critically and creatively with accepted ideas from the past.

Step 1: **Select.** Ask playwrights to select and bring to the workshop a classic play they know well.

Step 2: **Describe.** In brief presentations, writers summarize the plays and explain how the endings resolve dramatic action and complete thematic meaning for the play.

Step 3: **Read.** Read aloud Tom Stoppard's *15-Minute Hamlet* and *Cahoot's Macbeth*.

Step 4: **Discuss.** What is Stoppard doing in these adaptations of Shakespeare's plays? How do ideas in Stoppard's work relate to themes in Shakespeare's plays?

Step 5: **Rewrite.** Playwrights either rewrite the endings of the classics they've brought to the workshop, changing not only what happens, but also what it means – or they write a much shortened version of the classic play emphasizing one aspect of the original.

Step 6: **Read.** Pass out copies of the new endings and short plays so that participants can read all the parts while the playwright listens.

Step 7: **Discuss.** How does the new ending affect the meaning of the original? Compare endings of the classic and adaptation – which is more compelling, disturbing, surprising? Which ending would you prefer to see in a production?

◆◆◆

Playwright Perspective:
Kirk Lynn

"I let anything I write be a play. Or be a text for performance."

Were you an original member of the Rude Mechanicals and if not, how did you get involved with the company?

Sure. I wrote a play called *Pale Idiot* and a lot of people liked it. Most of these people were fresh off a theatrical break up. They were trying to form a Shakespeare Company and when voting on a name the men in the company rigged the vote so that the name the women liked, Rude Mechanicals, wouldn't win. This was discovered and the whole deal was off. So some of these women liked my play, *Pale Idiot*, and we decided to form a theatre company. I think the original idea was to produce a few of my plays and a lot of Shakespeare's plays.

But when Shawn Sides came back to Texas from NYU and created her thesis project, a devised version of *Taming of the Shrew...* well then... the Rude Mechs knew who it was, I think this was three productions in... Or two. I know they did *Pale Idiot* and it was a big success. I remember building a giant set out of donated cardboard. I remember paying a guy $50 bucks to play the bongos for each show. I remember doing a command performance for the local critic who had missed it...

How does your process in writing fit with the Rude Mechanical process of creating new work?

I don't know that it does. I think my process of living and being a friend fits with the Rude Mechs' process of creating new work. My process of writing is to sit down and write. To try to follow my whims. I read this Bruce Nauman quote once about his decision to allow anything he did in his studio to be art, for him and it freed him up in some way. So I let anything I write be a play. Or be a text for performance. Recently I was giving myself the freedom to write plays that had no actors or text or sets or anything. Like

149

performance scripts for life... and an idea that came to me was to recreate my entire sexual history with my wife and to recreate hers with me. That we would perform them on and with and for each other, the good and the bad. This was writing, mind you, not doing it... But the idea that any two people might do this for and with one another was a day's work... and then many weeks later I decided to write that as the plot of a traditional play... with characters... and that became *Your Mother's Copy of the Kama Sutra*, which is at Playwrights Horizons next season.

So when I am trying to do something as and for the Rude Mechs, I try to be just as free, but there are several people who want things, myself included. I try to make scenes the artistic directors want to perform. I try to match my time and whims to their time and whims. In this last piece, *Stop Hitting Yourself,* Lana brought in Ayn Rand's *Anthem* as an inspiration, maybe two weeks into rehearsals, and I already had at least two other narratives and plays that didn't have much to do with *Anthem*... but it was rich material in the room, so the part of me that wants to live with the Rude Mechs in my life forever and the part of me that loves and trusts the other Rudes as friends and artists said, SURE and tried to translate what I was doing to their desires. And it worked great.

But I don't think writing suits devising, by and large, I think they are an odd fit, and I think that is why it can be so exciting sometimes. Like David Byrne in that big suit... The Rude Mechs is much bigger than all of us, so having some little person in it at any moment, directing or writing or whatever can make an exciting weird picture...

I think if you want *Streetcar*, writing with a collective is not going to be an efficient system for making something like that... but if you want the *Constitution* or *Dionysus in 69* or *Midsummer*, then it's a good system...

KIRK LYNN *is a playwright and Co-Producing Artistic Director of the Austin-based, experimental theater collective Rude Mechanicals (or Rude Mechs). Lynn co-founded the Rude Mechs in 1995 and, with them, he has written and adapted over a dozen plays, which have been performed around the world. His works have been honored with several awards, including the Total Theatre Award from the Edinburgh Fringe Festival for* Get Your War On *(2007) and an NEA New Play Development grant for* I've Never Been So Happy *(2009). In 2011 he received a fellowship grant from United States Artists, and he currently teaches at the University of Texas, Austin.*

◆ ◆ ◆

Through performance, this debate about the meaning of theatre, and how it structures representations of our culture might enter the lives and imaginations of a much larger community.
— Jill Dolan, *Geographies of Learning*

One way for playwrights to seek new forms is simply to leave playwriting behind, or at least conventional ideas of what a play is or playwriting should be. Life is full of events and activities that aren't normally considered theatre but can be seen as a kind of performance: they are interesting to view – they have unique environs, something happens, things change – they create relationships between observer and observed, and they beg a closer examination and interpretation of what might be going on and what that might mean.

Theatre vérité? Not necessarily. Theatre not only reflects life, it appropriates life. In an ongoing effort to keep current and remain relevant, the theatre begs, borrows, and steals ideas and artifacts anywhere it finds them. Here are instances of appropriation that have endured the test of cultural fad to become standard forms of expression in American theatre. Starting in the 1960s, thanks to the work of the National Theatre of the Deaf, American Sign Language became one of the standard ways actors and audiences communicate. In the 1970s, competitive sports entered the stage via Theatresports, which combines traditional theatre improvisation with techniques used in professional wrestling. There are also dramatic genres that have for decades or centuries annexed inspiration and content from other literary forms: theatre of the novel (adaptation), theatre of the interview (docudrama), and theatre of journalism (living newspaper).

This creative commingling helps to keep theatre artistically vital, socially current, and politically relevant. With such important benefits, the question becomes: Why isn't there more commingling? Why isn't there a theatre of social media, a theatre of gaming, of DNA genome, of food, of monsters, of travel? Those subjects are dealt with now and again, though less often on stage than on television, where some of them have found a sizeable following.

The four projects outlined in this section look beyond the realm of theatre for inspiration: graphic novels, music CDs, visual art, and the Supreme Court. In each case, the playwright's challenge is to recognize and exploit the theatricality inherent in a completely separate artistic medium or political process. A good place to begin is to look at the topic at hand and simply ask, "Why isn't this considered theatre? How could a playwright respond to this and create a text for performance?"

◆ ◆ ◆

Graphic/Audio: Divide and Conquer

I really like books that you can kind of hear as much as think about, that are so graphic and visual.
– Laurie Anderson, *Interview, Silicon Valley Radio*

In traditional productions audiences rely on sight and sound to experience fully a live performance. Occasionally the senses of smell, taste, and touch are involved, as well as the need to move about an untraditional space. *Fefu and Her Friends* was penned by Marie Irene Fornes with audience mobility in mind, and Punchdrunk labeled its production of *Sleep No More* a new kind of "immersive theatre in which roaming audiences experience epic storytelling inside sensory theatre worlds."

This is not to suggest that food, odors, fingers, and ambulation should be added to Aristotle's six elements of drama. In fact, to heighten the theatricality of a new play, quite the opposite is true – at least in terms of process. By isolating and emphasizing a single sense above the others – as audio plays do with hearing and graphic plays do with seeing – a play appeals more directly to audience imaginations because more of the overall event is implied and less is illustrated.

Of course, an audience's experience is significantly affected by the medium through which a play is delivered. This means that one script becomes two quite different events when translated into two different media. Playwrights who adapt their conventional stage plays as audio and graphic plays often make bold choices to maximize the theatrical assets of the other media. They also tend to reduce spoken text because pictures and sounds speak volumes. And, since audio and graphic plays are less familiar forms than conventional stage plays, playwrights discover they must invent more and assume less. This lack of familiarity breeds creativity, which can lead to bold theatrical strokes and streamlined narratives.

WORKSHOP: AUDIO AND GRAPHIC PLAYS

In this workshop, playwrights begin with a conventional script for a stage play. When they complete the audio and graphic script adaptations, it's time to assess new ideas, images, and metaphors that have been created and to re-evaluate original text that proved unnecessary in other media. When returning to the original stage play, the question a playwright should ask is: What additions, revisions, and deletions might be incorporated from these sight and sound explorations? The goal of this workshop is to encourage bold and unusual theatrical choices through a process of isolation, emphasis, and re-integration.

WORKSHOP: THE URTEXT

Step 1: **Write.** Each playwright writes or brings to the workshop a short play five-to-ten minutes in length.

Step 2: **Read.** Participants read all the roles in each play so the playwrights can listen.

Step 3: **Analyze.** Discuss the main action, characters, theme, and theatricality (What will enliven the play in terms of sight, sound, and action in performance?)

WORKSHOP: AUDIO ADAPTATION

Step 1: **Listen.** There are numerous audio plays on the Internet; check out BBC Radio Plays, Orson Welles's *War of the Worlds*, Twilight Zone Radio, and Finalrune Productions.

Step 2: **Analyze.** How do the audio performances capitalize on the use of sounds other than speech? What sound effects differ from what you'd expect in a stage production of the play? What about silence and tempo of dialogue?

Step 3: **Adapt**. Writers adapt their stage plays as audio plays; first as scripts and then as recorded productions with actors and sound effects. Encourage writers to create as complete a world as possible and to incorporate non-realistic sounds that add metaphor, suspense, or atmosphere.

Step 4: **Read, listen, discuss**. Listen to the audio recording and compare it with the reading of the original script. How does sound create location, image, idea? How was sound used differently than described in the original stage play? Was all of the original text necessary – was any of it deleted or replaced by sound effects?

WORKSHOP: GRAPHIC ADAPTATION

Step 1: **Read.** You should have no problem finding interesting graphic novels (three of the best are *Perspolis* by Marjane Satrapi, *Gods' Man, A Novel in Woodcuts* by Lynn Ward, and *Maus: A Survivor's Tale, Volumes 1 and 2* by Art Spiegelman); graphic classics like *Moby Dick, Macbeth* and *King Lear*; and Japanese manga and American comic books.

Step 2: **Analyze**. What is the spatial ratio of image to text? What kinds of things do the visual images convey (action, emotion, location, mood)? How is text used (dialogue, thoughts, narration)? How important to the reader's experience are perspective and scale?

Step 3: **Introduce.** There are numerous ways to create a graphic text that don't require much artistic talent. Writers can add captions or text to images by using photo caption programs on-line. Students can take photos of actors on location using close-ups and angles, use found images, or draw their own. Sometimes simple and primitive images are most effective. Ask writers to storyboard their visual ideas before tackling the adaptation.

Step 3: **Adapt**. Writers adapt their original scripts as graphic plays using their storyboards as guides. Allow a week or two for this creative process.

Step 4: **Read and discuss**. Spend a class passing around and reading the graphic plays. Compare graphic adaptations with original texts. Has text been reduced? Have visual metaphors and motifs appeared? Does reader response to an emphasis on visual imagery differ significantly from the audience experience of a stage performance?

WORKSHOP: REVISING THE URTEXT

Step 1: **Consider.** What has been learned that might be incorporated from the sight and sound explorations?

Step 2: **Revise.** Write a new draft of the original text incorporating as many ideas and elements from the audio/graphic plays as useful. Revisions don't need to incorporate new elements precisely; rather, aspects of the audio/graphic plays may inspire different changes to the original (an entire soundscape, perhaps, or visual metaphors).

Step 3: **Read**. Participants read all the roles while the playwright (and others) listen.

Step 4: **Discuss**. How does the revised draft of the stage play compare with the original? How did the audio/graphic explorations inform the revision? Which medium (audio, graphic, stage) seems best suited to the action and ideas of the play?

◆◆◆

AUDIO AND GRAPHIC PLAYS

The following two versions of *Carrion* by Valerie Smith were created for a course at Goucher College. The two scripts demonstrate how the process of adapting a stage play for audio and graphic media leads to different theatrical expressions for the two media. Note the emphasis on the sound of flapping wings in the audio version, the importance of posture and perspective in the graphic version, and different ways that dialogue is emphasized.

CARRION: An Audio Play
by Valerie Smith

Cast
    Heather
    Gary
    GPS Voice
    Buzzard

(Silence. Rising sound of a desert wind, whistling eerily and increasing in volume. It's like eternity blowing through your brain. Suddenly, the weird scream of the buzzard, amplified and echoing, which morphs into the high-pitched whine of a car engine on the blink. Perhaps some grinding sounds, some engine coughing, hiccupping. Silence. The maddening "neh-neh-neh" sound of a stalled engine that almost turns over...but then doesn't. This, three times, each becoming slower and more labored, until the inevitable "clunk" of the ignition with no response. Silence. Clunk. More silence. Clunk. More silence. Clunk. Then clunk. Clunk. Clunk. Death. Silence. Sound of car doors being opened, two sets of feet climbing out of the car onto desert gravel. Foot steps on desert

gravel going away then coming back.

The sound of the wind continues subtly in the background throughout.)

GARY: Well. This blows.

HEATHER: I know I shouldn't ask but…

GARY: Oh…where are we? Well, according to the GPS, we are .26 miles from a major downtown shopping center. Which, unless somehow we missed the nuclear blast, I can only think is NOT RIGHT. The GPS led us astray.

HEATHER: How is that possible?! It's brand new. Dad gave it to me for Christmas!

GARY: Oh, well then! Everything's great! The car is completely dead but I'll just stroll on over to the Shell station there and ask for help. And on the way back, I'll pick us up a couple of venti iced lattis at that convenient Starbucks while you go shopping.

HEATHER: Ah!

GARY: Well, what do you want me to say, Heather? Look at this moonscape! We're kinda screwed here! Jesus God, it's hot out here.

HEATHER: *(Overlapping)* Oh c'mon Gary. *(Sound of cellphone buttons being pushed.)* Let's not panic. We'll call somebody and they'll come and help us. I'll call 911 and you call…the National Guard or something….

GARY: *(Sound of more cell buttons being pushed.)* Oh, yes! That number is seared into memory! How 'bout we call your dad…tell him how your Christmas present is working out?

HEATHER: You can be such jerk sometimes.

(Silence. And…more silence.)

GARY: Shit. I'm not getting a signal. Are you getting a signal? *(Pause)* Heather?

(Sounds of cellphone buttons being pushed.)

Heather? Heather?

(The sound of Heather clamoring up onto the car.)

Are you getting anything? *(Pause.)* You're not getting anything. Stop waving your arm around! Okay? Come down from there. Please. Heather. *(Pause.)* Heather, wha-the-fu, Heather get off the top of the car! Admit it! Admit you are not getting a signal either!

> *(The sound of Heather climbing down off the car.)*

HEATHER: You are really being a jerk, Gary!

GARY: *(Overlapping)* Okay, okay...I'm sorry, alright? I'm sorry!

HEATHER: Fine!

GARY: It's just so...damn hot out here.

HEATHER: Well, it doesn't help anything to yell at me.

GARY: I...fine. I apologize. Okay?

HEATHER: I was sort of getting a signal...

GARY: What does that mean? "... sort of getting a signal..." Either you were or you weren't....

HEATHER: *(Overlapping)* I was getting a few bars, Gary... not much but it's significant...

GARY: That's not a signal! That's just to torture us! We can't reach anybody with that!

HEATHER: Nothing you say is going to make me lose hope.

> *(Silence. The sound of the wind. The buzzard call is closer now.)*

GARY: Heather. There are no cell phone towers here. There are no satellites that beam here. Look around you. *THERE IS NOTHING HERE, HEATHER. Nothing. We are – in a word –* screwed.

HEATHER: I see a bird up there, Gary. Hope is a thing with feathers.

> *(Silence. The wind. The buzzard calls louder as it circles, an eerie reverberating squawk.)*

GARY: Heather, that bird up there?

HEATHER: What?...

GARY: Do you know what a buzzard is?

HEATHER: Gary...

GARY: Do you? Do you know what a buzzard is? Oh, and look it's circling. Do you know why it's doing that, Heather?

HEATHER: *(Overlapping)* Gary! Yes, I know what a buzzard is, Mr....Mr.....Glass Half-Empty! It might not be a buzzard. It could be a hawk or a....a...peregrine falcon!

GARY: *(Pause.)* A peregrine falcon?

HEATHER: Gawd! I don't know! Why are we talking about a stupid bird?! We should be formulating a plan! But no, let's mope around! Or better, let's blame Heather! "Oh, we're so helpless! We're just lame, hopeless little human beings who have no ability to be proactive or think through a situation to a solution! We might as well just curl up and die now! Oh, we're screwed! Perfect!"

(Silence.)

GARY: Okay. Point taken. So...what's our plan?

HEATHER: I'm just saying we should...start being more positive. Instead of standing around and...instead of standing around.

GARY: I'm all for that. Where do we start?

HEATHER: *(Pause.)* Okay. *(Pause.)* Okay! Well, first thing to do when confronting a problem is, let's ask are there any obvious solutions? Maybe it's staring us in the face and we just have to...see it. Right. Sort of like when you send something to the printer and it doesn't print and you assume that it's a network problem so you go to all the trouble of calling I. T. Admin and they try everything and absolutely NOTHING is working. So...you visit the printer...and you discover that some duff-bot cleaning person unplugged the damned thing to vacuum and never plugged it back in. *(Pause.)* Sort of like that.

GARY: Right. So....

HEATHER: So we...we look under the hood! Maybe something just...came...loose!

GARY: All right. I'm game. *(The sound of their footsteps moving to the car. The sound of the hood being released, then raised. A long silence.)* Jee-zus!

HEATHER: Wow.

GARY: What happened to distributor caps? Look at that thing. When did car engines morph into alien space ships...on crack?

HEATHER: It was an option, Gar.

GARY: It was a thought.

HEATHER: Exactly.

GARY: *(Exploding)* Christ, it's hot out here! What are we gonna do?! What the hell do we do now?! This is a nightmare! Of untold proportions! I feel...completely... IMPOTENT!

HEATHER: *(Overlapping)* Gary. Gary. Gar—I know. I know. It's gonna be all right. Calm down. Honey. We'll work this out, we will. We have to.

GARY: How?! How are we going to work this out?!

HEATHER: It's okay, honey. Breathe.

GARY: I'm so hot I'm about to pass out.

HEATHER: Here. Sit here in the shade. That's it. Breathe. Deep breaths.

GARY: Gawd, I could use a nice cold smoothie right now. Even if it was a green tea smoothie. I'd even drink that. If it had ice in it.

HEATHER: I know. A smoothie would be good. That's it. Just relax. We'll be okay, honey. Okay?

GARY: Yeah. I'm sorry, hon. I guess I just don't...respond as well to crisis situations as you do.

HEATHER: That's okay, Gar. We just have to stay positive. And keep thinking. 'Kay?

GARY: 'Kay.

> *(Silence. The sound of wings fluttering. The buzzard emits a low chuckle.)*

HEATHER: Gar?

GARY: Yeah?

HEATHER: Ohhhhhhhh. Ohhhhhhhh. OHHHHHHHHH!

GARY: What? What?

HEATHER: Oh yes! Yes! I feel a brain-wave comin' on!

GARY: What? Heather? What...?

163

(The sound of HEATHER rooting around in the car.)

HEATHER: Ohmigod! I DID bring it! YES!

GARY: Heather?

HEATHER: This, Gary my love, is a TS9 connector, a 6-Band antenna, and an 825 Aircard! *(Pause.)* No, look. If you can get any kind of location on the GPS, figure out where we are, I can plug in the Aircard to the laptop, hook the connector to the antenna and plug those in, and presto! We can boost the signal, that little signal, and EMAIL for help! It just could maybe work! *(Pause.)* Thank you, Daddy! *(Pause.)* Suddenly, there is god.

GARY: Ohh-kayy.

HEATHER: I'll just boot this....Well, go on, jump in that front seat and see what you can raise, Gar, my darling... find out where we are!

GARY: Fine! We'll do this thing. We're gonna do this. Yes.

HEATHER: Yes!

(Multiple sounds of technology being raised. The chime of a laptop being booted. The beep of a GPS coming on.)

GARY: Ouch! Ouuue! Hot buttons! Please don't be fried! Please work. Please. Okay. Positive. Press this little thingie...here...

GPS: Recalculating....

GARY: Yes! Recalculating! It's recalculating. *(Calling out.)* Heather, it's recalculating!

HEATHER: That's great, honey!

GPS: Yuccaville, 2.5 miles.

GARY: Heather! I think we're near a town called Yucca-ville!

HEATHER: Yuckyville. Got it! Great! Yes! Google! Yes! Email! Okay...

GPS: Turn right at Lombard Street, go .45 miles...

GARY: Lombard Street!

HEATHER: Right!

GPS: Take roundabout to Exit 2 to Sussex, 1.5 kilometers…

GARY: Wha…? What the fu…? We're in England now?

HEATHER: *(Sound of typing on laptop.)* Dear Daddy, The GPS…totally…betrayed us…the car is broken…we're in the…desert….and it's really hot…and our cell phones don't work…and we…are stuck…in the middle of… nowhere….Near…Yuckyville? Gary…is…freaking. We desperately need you to call the National Guard….or whatever…to fly over and get us out of here…Ah…it's really, REALLY hot, Dad. We could…die. Please email back…and let me know…that you…got this. *(Pause.)* P. S. I'm using the great Signal Booster kit you gave me! Thank you! *(Pause.)* 'Kay-y-y-y. Now. SEND! Sweet. Little circle thingie going round.

GPS: Recalculating…

GARY: Yeah. You better recalculate, you…

GPS: Recalculating…

GARY: No, Gary. Stay calm. Positive thoughts…'Member. BE POSITIVE.

GPS: Recalculating…

GARY: What about Yuccaville! Where did that go? C'mon!

GPS: Recalculating…

GARY: Oh, this is just bull…

GPS: Congratulations! You have arrived!

GARY: …CRAP! You bastard! You incompetent, treacherous piece of technological pigswill…

> *(Sound of crunching as Gary flings the GPS to the gravel and jumps on it, stomping it into oblivion. The buzzard cackles and screeches.)*

HEATHER: Little circle STILL going round. And round. And round. And round. COME! ON! YOU HAVE TO SEND THE MESSAGE! SEND THE…FREAKIN'… MESSAGE! I, HEATHER, COMMAND YOU! NOW! ON PAIN OF DEATH! (Pause.) I HATE YOU! I HATE YOUIHATEYOUIHATEYOU!

(Sound of Heather going ballistic, jumping up and down on the laptop. The cracking and popping of plastic. The buzzard screams, near and immediate. Suddenly silence. A long pause. The wind blows.)

GARY: Heather?

HEATHER: Gary? *(Pause.)* Ohmigod, Gary. What have we done? Omigod!

GARY: It's okay, Heather.

HEATHER: *(She is crying.)* Omigod, what did we just do? Omigod! We just destroyed, like, thousands of dollars of high-end electronics. We're going to die out here, and shrivel and be eaten by animals. Omigod! Omigod!

GARY: Breathe, honey. Breathe.

HEATHER: Omigod! This never happens to me. Look at me. I'm shaking, Gar. I'm shaking. Look at my hands.

GARY: Calm down, honey. Calm down. We're gonna do what we should have done to begin with.

HEATHER: Wha?...

GARY: We're gonna start walking...

HEATHER: Omigod, Gary. LEAVE THE CAR?

GARY: Yes, honey, leave the car and follow our tracks back to the main road...

HEATHER: Omigod! Leave the car...

GARY: *(Overlapping.)* No, now, it's the only solution. Hope, remember? We have to hope. There's lots of tire tracks back there, people doing that...off-road...thingie that people do...

HEATHER: Omigod...we're doomed.

GARY: No, now, we're not doomed. We're bound to bump into somebody...this is America, there is no privacy. But I have to have you on board. Are we together on this, sweetheart? We'll be okay, okay? Okay? Heather? Okay?

HEATHER: *(Reluctantly)* Okay.

GARY: That's the spirit! That's my Heather! *(Making light of it.)* Huh-ho! Wow, Heather, look at that Mac, wow. You really off-loaded your grump on that thing! Huh?

HEATHER: *(Sniffing.)* Well. *(Sniff.)* Yeah. *(Sniff.)* It WAS incredibly satisfying.

GARY: Yes, yes, it was. *(Pause.)* Okay then. Let's get going.

HEATHER: *(Sadly)* 'Bye car.

> *(Their footsteps travel off into the distance. The sound of the wind of eternity rising. The buzzard's scream comes closer, echoing, the sound of its wings become the wind.)*

THE END

VAL SMITH'S *plays have been produced in the Humana Festival of New American Plays and the Classics in Context Festival at Actors Theatre of Louisville. Her ten-minute plays and full-lengths for adults and young audiences are published by Samuel French, Smith & Kraus, and Dramatic Publishing.*

Carrion: A Graphic Play
by Valerie Smith

Nehhhhhhhhhhhhhhhhhhhhhpock....nehhhhhhhhhhhhhhhhhhhhhpockitapockita...nehhhhhhhhhhhhhhhhhhhhh-pockita...nehhhhhhhhhhhhhhhhhhhhhpockitapockita...nehhhhhhhhhhhhhhhhhhhhhhpockita....pock...pock... pock...nehhhhhh, nehhhhhh, nehhhhhh, clunk. Nehhhh, nehhhhhhh, nehhhhhhh, clunk. Nehhhhh, nehhhh, clunk. Nehhhhhh...nehhhhh....nehhhhhhhhhhhhhhhhhhhhhh-h-h-h--h---h------h-----h. Clunk. Clunk.

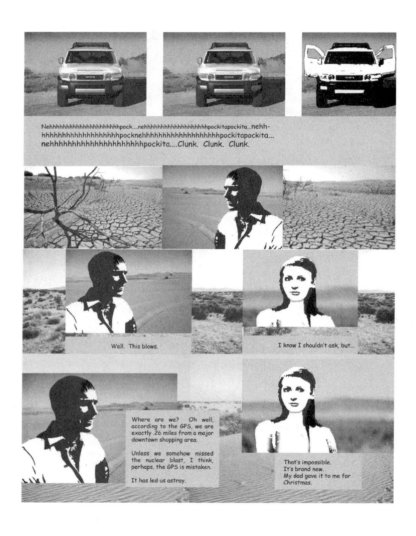

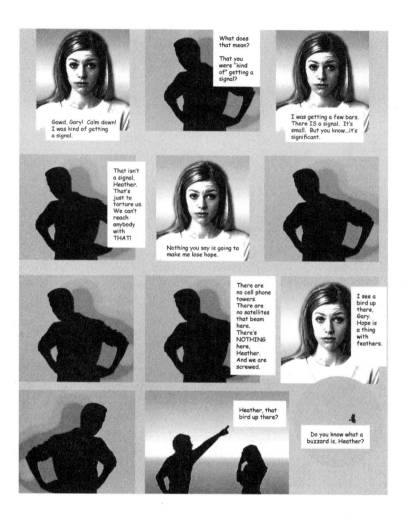

173

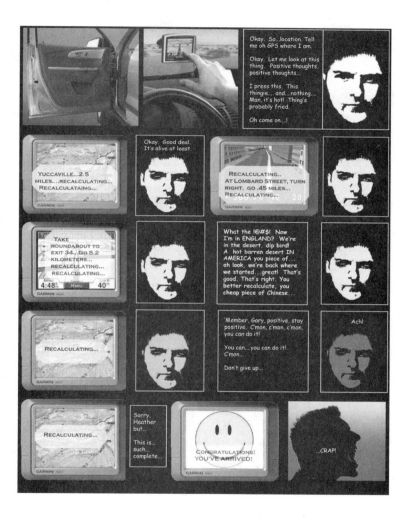

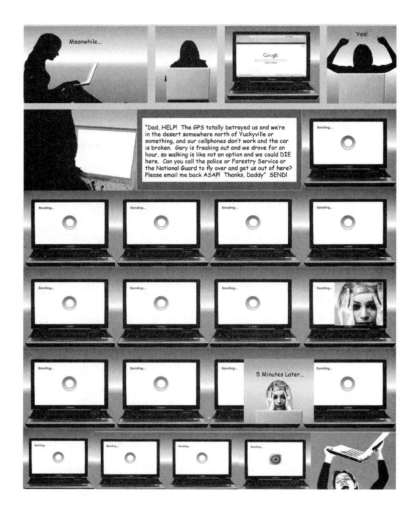

179

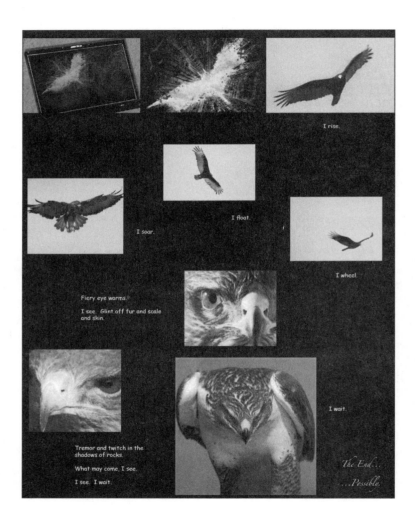

I rise.

I float.

I soar.

I wheel.

Fiery eye warms.

I see. Glint off fur and scale
and skin.

I wait.

Tremor and twitch in the
shadows of rocks.

What may come, I see.

I see. I wait.

The End...

...Possibly.

Jukebox Musical Challenge

Ninety-nine percent of the world's lovers are not with their first choice. That's what makes the jukebox play.

– Willie Nelson,
The Tao of Willie: A Guide To Happiness in Your Heart

The musical is America's great contribution to non-realistic theatre, and its worldwide popularity proves (as if proof were needed!) that audiences take great pleasure in performance virtuosity and pure theatricality in the service of dramatic storytelling. Since music is one, if not the, primary artistic expression of our culture, the musical provides an appealing genre for writers who want to experiment with the creative methods outlined in this book. Obviously, not all playwrights are musically gifted, so this workshop is designed to let writers play with the structural and narrative aspects of musicals without needing to compose music or write lyrics.

The jukebox musical is comprised of existing popular songs that may be presented as a revue or worked into a storyline, sometimes a biography of a musician or members of a musical group (*Fela!*, *Jersey Boys*, and *Love, Janis*), and sometimes an original story or adaptation (*Mamma Mia!* and *Forbidden Planet*). Two variations on the musical have appeared on Broadway in recent years. In *Movin' Out*, Twyla Tharp told a story through modern dance choreographed to the songs of Billy Joel, which were played and sung by a band separate from the dancers. Also, director John Doyle employed actor-musicians who accompanied themselves in *Company* and *Sweeney Todd, The Demon Barber of Fleet Street* – there was no other orchestra.

Given the theatrical appeal of music, there is no reason other than tradition that a musical needs to follow the rules of realistic drama. The story need not be told in chronological order or feature consistent characters or be set in recognizable locations. In fact, there needn't be a story at all, just a unifying concept

181

such as the music of Eubie Blake in *Eubie!* or Fats Waller in *Ain't Misbehavin'*. Given the freedoms of the form, the jukebox musical is an ideal genre in which to experiment with all kinds of non-realistic constructs, especially division, bricolage, and altered states as described elsewhere in this volume.

WORKSHOP: JUKEBOX MUSICAL CHALLENGE

This workshop asks writers as librettists to bend, stretch, shuffle, and subvert conventional dramatic structures and techniques so that a pre-determined sequence of songs on an album can be reconceived as the music and lyrics for a jukebox musical. By working with the songs as they're sequenced on the album, students need to create a theatrical event and/or dramatic journey from something that was conceived as a listening experience or concert. To succeed in this translation from music to musical, the writers/librettists will need to make outrageous, irrational, surprising choices that can, for example, transform folk ballads into show-stopping eleven o'clock numbers, emphasize the irony in sentimental love songs, create surreal moments with singing objects, or re-contextualize the songs by having them sung by an incongruous character or community (e.g., Mary Kay salespeople, aliens, Bill Moyers, or the Lost Boys from the Sudan). The aim of the workshop is to encourage writers to look beyond causality and rationality for theatrical inspiration.

Step 1: **Select.** To get started, each writer finds an album that features music and lyrics by a performer or band with whom the writer is *not* familiar, and preferably someone who's not famous and whose work is not well known. Also, it's important that most, if not all, of the song tracks include lyrics. Searching through stacks of used CDs and LPs in second-hand stores is a great way to discover overlooked and unusual talent.

Step 2: **Review.** There are some basic principles that can help students construct a musical from a series of songs. Once writers have made their album selections, the second step is to review the musical notes that follow from playwright/librettist/lyricist Janet Allard.

Step 3: **Create.** Playwrights will conceive and author the book for a jukebox musical incorporating all the songs on the album. Writers must:

- use the songs in the order they appear on the album.
- avoid relying on realistic conventions of causality, linear chronology, and obvious locations. In other words, things can happen without clear causes, time can be jumbled or is irrelevant, characters needn't be human, and locations can be imaginary, impossible, or highly unusual.
- experiment with some of the concepts in this volume, such as division, distortion, anthropomorphism, or bricolage.
- and apply as many of Janet Allard's guidelines as possible.

Step 4: **Take your time.** Creative breakthroughs require time and experimentation, so allow at least a week for writer imaginations to run wild with possibilities. When playwrights rush, they tend to rely on instincts rather than taking the time to dream up and consider new possibilities. And our instincts, of course, have been conditioned by conventions of realism.

Step 5: **Read.** Participants read the librettos aloud in class, playing the songs on the albums at the appropriate times, while the playwright and others listen.

Step 6: **Analyze and discuss.** Did the jukebox musical hold your attention? Was the book as interesting as the lyrics and music (or more)? Was the event compelling and, if there was a journey or unifying theme, was it clear? How inventive was the writer's concept, and did the non-realistic devices add interest?

◆ ◆ ◆

JANET ALLARD: MUSICAL NOTES

When things are too great to speak, you sing, too great to sing, you dance. Build your scenes to the point where speaking isn't enough for the characters, they must sing.

"Words make you think. Music makes you feel. A song makes you feel a thought." – Yip Harburg. Songs do something the libretto can't do. A good libretto will feel incomplete without the songs.

Leave room for the music. Just as great lines of dialogue leave room for actors to act, so do great librettos leave room for the songs to do the majority of the emotional work.

Musicalize the most dramatic or emotional moments of your story.

Don't retread the same ground. Let your book scene do something different than the song does. If the song is the moment they fall in love, have the scene be the struggle that comes before that, or something else, as long as it doesn't repeat the same information or dramatic moment.

Let the songs be the star of your show. Remember, people leave musicals singing songs. The book is the structure that holds these songs together.

Intercut music and dialogue. Try interjecting lines of dialogue in the musical breaks. Does that help create a scene within a song?

"Let's sing our way out of this." – Elizabeth Fraire. Remember, singing is action. Allow the songs to move the story forward.

"If I cannot fly, let me sing." – Stephen Sondheim. Singing is a way of flying. Often characters literally fly in musicals, sometimes they soar emotionally or in thought. Let them soar.

Create internal and external moments for your characters. Is the song private or public? External or internal? Can other characters onstage hear the song or is it an internal moment where your character is working through an emotion or choosing their next course of action?

Think visually. What's going on onstage? What are the characters physically doing during the song? Are they dancing? Are they washing a car? Is there a chorus of women in bathtubs? Or factory workers building cars? What is physically happening during the song?

Make use of "spectacle". How can your show be visually theatrical? This can be big – like flying. Or small, like a match lit in the dark.

Decide who is singing. Is this a solo? Can you turn it into a duet? How about a full company number?

Decide who is singing (part two); make unexpected choices. How does the meaning of the song change depending on who sings it? In the 2007 film *I'm Not There*, six actors (including Heath Ledger and Cate Blanchett) portray six personas of music legend Bob Dylan at various stages of his life – illustrating how Bob Dylan reinvented himself. In *Caroline, or Change* by Tony Kushner and Jeanine Tesori the singing characters include a washing machine, a dryer, a radio, the moon, a bus. Make interesting choices about who (or what) sings each song.

Choose your context. What happens if you put the song in an unexpected setting or context? "School House Rock" would be very different sung in a classroom by ten-year olds than in an old folks home. In the film *Across the Universe* (2007), Julie Taymor inserts Beatles songs against a dynamic backdrop of the Vietnam War.

Create a world where characters sing. This is either a theatrical world where characters sing to express themselves or there is some literal context. *A Closer Walk With Patsy Cline* uses the frame of a radio show. *Here Lies Love* by Fat Boy Slim and David Byrne casts the audience as partygoers at a dance club in the Philippines where a DJ spins the music.

Study the structure of a musical you love. Many, many musicals in the American theater have a very similar structure. Take one of your favorite musicals and listen to each song – break it down – what is each song doing – you may be surprised that they follow a similar pattern. Follow the pattern/structure of one of your favorite musicals.

Steal from the best. Here are some things historically included in many many musicals. You can include them in yours:
- A full company "opening number" that establishes the "world" of the show. Who are we? Where are we? What do we do? This can also establish a theme – "Tradition" from *Fiddler on the Roof* does this.
- An "I want" song – Your main character hopes for something here. It becomes evident who we, the audience are following. Who are they and what do they want? They somehow stand out from (or in opposition to) the world they live in.
- A duet or love song. Musicals often have a love story.
- Opening of act two – sometimes this is a full company number; it gets the audience back into the show.
- 11 o'clock number – sometimes the second to last number in a musical – or at least late in the second act. This is a show-stopping powerhouse of a number. Listen to "Rose's Turn" from *Gypsy* and you'll understand what an 11 o'clock number is.

Go Big or Go Home. Musicals are great at telling big, epic stories. Allow your characters and your story to be larger than life.

Include Joy. Joy is an underexplored emotion in naturalistic playwriting. Musicals do joy well. Even Sweeney Todd experiences joy. Joy is contagious.

JANET ALLARD *is an award-winning playwright and book-writer/lyricist. Her musical credits include* Pool Boy *with composer Niko Tsakalakos (Barrington Stage, 2010) and* The Unknown: a silent musical, *which won a Jonathan Larson Award (P73 productions, 2002; The Public Theater's New Work Now Festival, 2004; the New York Musical Theater Festival, 2005). Her play* Vrooommm! A NASComedy *premiered in Ariel Tepper's Summer Play Festival in NYC, and her work has been seen at the Guthrie, The Kennedy Center, Mixed Blood, Playwrights Horizons, Yale Rep, The Yale Cabaret, The Women's Project and internationally in Ireland, England, Greece, Australia and New Zealand. She attended the Graduate Musical Theatre Writing Program at NYU and teaches at UNC-Greensboro.*

◆ ◆ ◆

Ekphrastic Drama

"To write a well-made problem play or a witty comedy of manners may therefore be more laborious or require a higher degree of ingenuity or intelligence. On the other hand, to invent a generally valid poetic image of the human condition requires unusual depth of feeling and intensity of emotion, and a far higher degree of genuinely creative vision – in short, inspiration."
— Martin Esslin, *The Theatre of the Absurd*

For playwrights, there are two distinct approaches to formal innovation: 1) start with fundamentals of Aristotelian drama and push hard against the boundaries until they bend or break, or 2) start somewhere completely different and find what's theatrical in that other art form or genre. This ekphrastic project takes the second route.

Let's begin with an example: a project that began beyond the pale of conventional drama. *The Medium* was created two decades ago by the SITI Company and was directed by Anne Bogart, who wrote in her program notes,

> I began thinking about the nature of theater and how it will survive in a world where the very nature of entertainment is constantly being redefined. Long a fan of media philosopher Marshall McLuhan, I decided to use his insights to create a theater piece about who we are becoming vis-a-vis the radical developments in technology that surround us.

As a playwright, how does one start with McLuhan without ending up with a traditional bio-drama? If you begin by thinking of dramatic arc, character development, conflict, crisis … you're on the wrong track. To create new forms that convey new content – an endeavor McLuhan would certainly appreciate – start with material that is considered non-dramatic. In the case of this SITI production, the text was composed of philosophical musings by McLuhan, who's known for snappy aphorisms like, "Diaper spelled backwards is repaid. Think about it."

Which brings us to ekphrasis – think about it.

In the discipline of rhetoric in ancient Greece, ekphrasis referred to one medium of art trying to convey the essence and form of another medium or, more simply, a verbal and sometimes dramatic attempt to describe something visual. This process – the translation of visual to verbal and back again – speaks directly to the art of playwriting, which translates action and psychology into structured dialogue and stage directions only to be made visual once again in production.

This workshop uses ekphrasis as an associative process that disregards conventions of realism. By responding in poetic fashion to a visual image, playwrights are freed from internalized patterns of playwriting partly because they think they're not creating dramatic text at all. But they are. Read on.

Workshop: Ekphrastic Plays

The goal of this workshop is to help playwrights experiment with new possibilities for writing dramatic text by examining the theatricality that emerges in their work when they write in another literary genre.

Step 1: **Introduce.** Explain the meaning of ekphrastic: one art form trying to describe another art form.

Step 2: **View images.** Visit a museum of art and let writers find their own painting, collage, or sculpture for inspiration. It doesn't matter if the image is abstract or realistic. Images can also be printed and posted or projected so that writers in the workshop space can select a work that intrigues them. Examples of ekphrastic poems written by W. H. Auden, William Carlos Williams, and others can be found at www.poets.org.

Step 3: **Respond and write.** After spending time with the image, writers should respond to the work in writing, emotionally rather than descriptively. Let the first impulse be poetic, work from feeling, don't think too much about it.

Step 4: **Read and respond.** Writers read their works aloud so that others can express their experience of hearing the work for the first time: what sparked interest, generated feeling, made a personal connection? Was there a journey, progression, accumulation? With what cumulative impression were the listeners left?

Step 5: **Rehearse.** Divide writers into small groups to stage each of the works as though they were written as theatre text rather than poems. Groups are free to interpret and adapt the works as monologues, duologues, dialogue, choral verse, or call and response. They may also create characters and incorporate music, movement, and objects, but they need to remain true to the text.

Step 6: **Present and discuss.** After groups perform their theatre pieces, discuss what was effective in each piece? How was it different from an Aristotelian text with characters, dialogue, action, and conflict? What qualities of the writing merit further exploration as theatrical text? How might those qualities inspire or be incorporated into longer works of theatre? Can you imagine a full-length performance in this form?

Step 7. **Reflect.** By starting with art forms distinctly different from drama (visual art and poetry), writers are forced to think outside the box of dramatic writing. Ask writers to reflect on their thought process in this exercise and compare that with the thought process of writing more conventional dramatic text.

◆ ◆ ◆

Ekphrastic Plays

These three scripts were written in response to images published here during a workshop in Cleveland led by playwright Eric Schmiedl. The workshop participants included members of the Cleveland Playwrights Unit, a group of playwrights supported by The Cleveland Play House. Also a faculty member of the MFA-in-Writing program at Spalding University in Louisville, Kentucky, Schmiedl uses this exercise with his graduate students. "If you want to break from the conventions of realism," explained Schmiedl, "it's advantageous to work in other genres because you're forced to think – and write – in new ways. You approach your own writing and theatre in general with new eyes and ears."

("Depth", DFK/Dixon Studios)

A Better Door
by George Brant

INITIAL RESPONSE TO "DEPTH"

She has drawn me away from what might be a perfect work of art. She stands in front of it, her back to me, blocking it from me with her half-naked form. The painting is blurry; she is not. Or rather her naked form is not; her clothing (the little she wears) is blurry as well, the same blurriness, abstractness as the painting. She is in focus, her naked back, the tightly pulled hair.

The hair. It would be different if her hair were unbound, spilling down her back. It would seem that she'd surrendered to the painting. Perhaps that would make me look at the painting more clearly, I'd wonder what was in the painting that made this beautiful woman surrender.

But no. The hair is tightly bound. She is considering the painting, she has not surrendered to it. Is she considering surrendering? Perhaps, but I'd lean toward no. I don't think surrender is in her nature.

And what is in her nature? All we have is a naked back. Hair. And a stance. A stance that is in control, that confronts the painting with its confidence, its superiority. A stance that will not bow down to anything, much less a painting.

And yet....the painting has made her stop. Stop in the act of nudity to consider it. Arrested in the act of nudity. Something vital has seized her attention, caused her to stand confronting it. But why so close? Why does she stand so close? It is a detail that has drawn her in, some detail, but it is a detail that she denies us, she stands directly in front of it, blocking it from view. We are missing the vital piece of the painting, that is why it blurs so in comparison.

And perhaps that then is her plan: to seize our attention away from the painting. Perhaps it is a competition and she has used all the power at her disposal: her white naked back, her tightly pulled hair, her occlusion of the painting's heart. She has made it impossible to look anywhere else.

She does so by hiding her face, as well. If we saw her smile, a tear, the painting would have won, we would have to look at it to see what had caused them. But we see nothing. Nothing but her.

DIRECTIONS THIS MIGHT GO IN:

Guy sitting on bench in museum, can't look at painting, engages with woman

Painted the painting for her – wondering what she thought

Instead of a painting, she's looking out a window onto the NYC skyline at night – blocking the Empire State Building.

Conversation between a director and his actress in her dressing gown after a performance about being less good – due to her brilliance, the play isn't coming through, the other actors look horrible – she's somehow standing apart from the play

GEORGE BRANT'S *plays include* Elephant's Graveyard, Grounded, The Mourners' Bench, *and* Three Voyages of the Lobotomobile. *A Core Writer at The Playwrights' Center, his scripts have been awarded the Kennedy Center's David Cohen National Playwriting Award, the Smith Prize and the Keene Prize for Literature. His works are published by Samuel French, Oberon Books, and Smith & Kraus.*

◆ ◆ ◆

("Out of the Box," DFK/Dixon Studios)

The Weight

by Susan Apker

First Response

Red, blood red, blotting out the sun. Heat scorched landscape, dappled with persistent, resistant scrub. Not a soul. Not a sound. But the gallows resonating with the weight of authority; the rightness of justice. A mesmerizing justice in a spare and lonely horizon. He cannot pass by without stopping to stare. At what? A body? A heart? A strawberry? A blank space filled with death.

It is night, perhaps, or early morning. Filled with the anticipation of a new day; awaiting life to fill the empty space – imaginary space. A hole. A shift in the universe. He has looked at that space so many times. Seen the bodies swinging in the hot breeze; felt the shift in the earth when the last twitch of life has left the meat sack. He no longer sees faces, just the weight of justice as he lowers the bodies to the floor.

Notes for Dramatization: This is the beginning of a short one-man piece.

> *Spare stage with the projection behind the actor of a gallows with the strawberry hanging from the end of a rope. It is a dimly lit staging; the lighting becoming progressively brighter throughout the show. A man walks on stage, stops and looks at the gallows, studying it from several angles. He walks downstage and begins.*

MAN: Everything should be evenly weighted to support the body of a man. Well, usually a man. Occasionally one of the fancy women might shoot somebody who stiffed her, so to speak. But judges were hardly ever inclined to kill a woman. Figuring, and rightly so, that the prick had it coming to him for skipping out without paying. And we all have to pay, one way or the other.

But I hated hanging women. *(The projection of the strawberry has changed to the body of a woman.)*

Got so I hated hanging anybody. Any. Body. *(The projection has changed back to a hanging strawberry.)*

There were hundreds of 'em. Most of 'em guilty, I guess.

(Handing bodies flash in the background; one, two, three bodies at a time.)

At first, they all died different. Some just dropped and died. The weight of justice snapping their necks like dried kindling.

And some twitched with life, 'til they hung like meat sacks.

Every once in a while, it just didn't work. The rope was too short, and the fellow only fell a few feet, kicking and screaming while I had to haul him up and drop him again. Making sure that this time, he died.

I made my living from people dying.

Don't get me wrong. It was, is a good job. Supported me and my family for years. There were plenty of outlaws then. And bank robbers, and murderers.

After awhile, I didn't even see their faces anymore. They were blotted out by the sun, or suffused with blood their heads would look like big old strawberries. Anything but a face.

(A projection of the strawberry hanging from a rope again.)

SUSAN APKER *has had numerous short plays produced across the country and is currently at work on her first full-length piece. She is also the creator and producer of "Heller Shorts" – a highly successful short play festival of original works in Tulsa, Oklahoma.*

◆ ◆ ◆

("Movement," DFK/Dixon Studios)

Turning Away
by Margaret Lynch

INITIAL RESPONSE

In the right hand corner at the top sits the moon, mottled face with dark and oh-so bright areas, an aura of light surrounding it. The background or perhaps the sky is also bright and light, not a dark night sky. It is turbulent with visible brush strokes surrounding and edging the figures, approaching and fleeing from them. In the left hand corner at the bottom there is a black-grey top hat with a black-white-gray spiral, perhaps straw, perhaps party favor springing from the crown. And now the figures that dominate the painting – why did I take so long to get to them? Why did I approach them sideways? A naked or at least barely clothed male figure bends over in the background, head bowed, all shaded, arms hanging down, but in motion, perhaps a swimming motion, though his legs and torso are straight. He is folded like a jack-knife. The motion is downward. In front of him there is another man, perhaps the same man, but clothed in a dark suit and bright white shirt blazoning from throat, breast plate, and wrists. He faces out toward us, but his face is also in shadow, though features of eyes, nose, mouth and beard are faintly visible. From his right side, three arms radiate outward at different angles, falling from 45 degrees to 0, straight and next to his ready and expectant body. The furthest arm and hand are done with the most transparent wash of watercolor or ink, and the arm and hand become more solid in appearance as they close in next to the body. But finally there are the hands – the most sharply drawn and realistic element in the painting – all three of them, perhaps they are even collage elements – photographs of a hand, cut, applied, and repeated. Line and brush stroke tie together moon, bending man, and ready-man in one mysterious movement.

REVISION (FOLLOWING WORK WITH DAVID HANSEN)

It's a recurring nightmare. It must be night time because the moon hangs low in the sky, its face mottled with dark and bright spaces. But the sky itself is bright. It could be day; a top hat dances at the edge of my vision with a straw spiraling from its crown. Still, it's not the warm-bright of day but a charged, dangerous bright with swirling undercurrents of darkness. I cannot bear to look at the scene full on, because I know that when I do, I will see him, clothed in a dark suit and bright white buttons, two of them, and bright white shirt blazoning from throat, breast plate, and wrists. His face will be in menacing shadow, his arm pulling in slow motion to wait, poised, close to his body. His hand waiting to touch mine, innocent prelude to something I do not want to remember. Hooded face, body, stripped of bright, white shirt and dark tailored suit poised like a jack-knife above me. Once I see him, if I see his face – too-bright light and too-dark shadows will collide and consume me.

MARGARET LYNCH *has been a member of the Playwrights Unit of The Cleveland Play House since 1996 and served as dramaturg for Great Lakes Theater from 1984 to 2002. An Ohio Arts Council Fellowship recipient, she has written seven full-length plays and commissioned works, including* Gilgamesh on the Crooked River, *a collaboration with composer Daniel Bernard Roumain.*

◆ ◆ ◆

Supreme Court Do-Over:
Social Practice Playwriting

...[T]he idea of performance or performativity has emerged as a possible organizing concept for a wider range of cultural, social, and political activities.
— Thomas Postlewait and Tracy C. Davis, *Theatricality*

In the beginning, there was no written text – just a space for performers and observers to do their thing. Then playwrights wrote words to be spoken and sung. Later, they added a few stage directions to clarify action, such as "Exit, pursued by a bear." In the 19th and 20th centuries, as theory and technology enabled realistic illusions and effects, some playwrights wrote extensive descriptions of settings, moods, and moments, and publishers included the stage manager's record of blocking in acting editions.

Here's a mid-century sample from *Harvey* by Mary Chase, Act I, Scene 2.

> *(Exits down* **L.** *From back* **C** *now comes CHUM-LEY, followed by SANDERSON and KELLY. CHUM-LEY goes to chair* **R** *of desk. KELLY crosses above table to* **R. C.** *office for CHUMLEY's hat and coat. SANDERSON goes to top of desk.)*

Specific-to-one-set stage directions are, fortunately, no longer common practice in published scripts. Playwrights (and publishers) have learned to leave most design choices and behavioral staging to their artistic collaborators. Some playwrights even challenge actors, directors, and designers with impossible or enigmatic stage directions, as Naomi Iizuka advises in her *Perspective,* and as Mac Wellman does in this stage direction from *Description Beggared: or The Allegory of Whiteness:* "(She makes the spider.)" Whatever behavior or movement Wellman's stage direction inspires, it's probably never the same in any two productions of the play.

204

The trend toward minimal stage directions raises questions about playwriting itself. If playwriting no longer requires detailed descriptions of behaviors and locations, isn't a logical next step a script that doesn't prescribe every spoken word? If a playwright leaves room for artistic interpretations, might that writer also leave space for audience contributions? And if a playwright collaborates on a production with a director, designers, and actors, might that same playwright also envision the audience as collaborators (more than observers and respondents) in the performance?

"Interactive experience" is a buzz-phrase of our age. Theatregoers have always "interacted" – applause, jeers, laughter, dead silence – response affects performance, we know. It's likely, however, that over the past several decades technological advances and cultural shifts have changed the audience more than the theatre. The experience of buying a ticket, taking a seat, and watching a performance from a darkened auditorium is no longer in the vanguard of interactive entertainment. There is no X-box for an audience watching most plays – especially realistic productions that follow a scripted course regardless of the ticket-buyers' response.

That is not to say that attending theatre is no longer a vibrant and meaningful experience in the 21st century. It certainly is in its way. But, when thinking about a public that craves creative interaction, how interactive really is the experience of watching a scripted performance from twelve rows back or the balcony?

Interest in audience/art interaction has fostered a movement called "social practice art," which Kate Taylor of the *New York Times* defines as an attempt "to blur the boundaries between creator and audience and encourage political engagement." In her article, Taylor refers to the New York City production of *City Council Meeting* as a prime example.

> *City Council Meeting* ... is performed not by actors, but by members of the audience. Upon arrival, they can volunteer to be a member; a speaker, who reads real testimony from one of the cities; a supporter, who is instructed by the staff to respond

205

positively to certain speakers; or a bystander, who gets to sit back and just observe.

The show is kept moving by the Council Secretary, who is a professional actress, and the staffers, a rotating group of non-professional actors who are part of each show... They have designated duties, including whispering instructions, both practical and not, in the members' ears. [*NYT*, May 9, 2013]

City Council Meeting co-creators Mallory Catlett, Jim Findlay, and Aaron Landsman based their exercise in "performed participatory democracy" on transcripts of public meetings in nine cities. They didn't shy away from the dull routine of those civic events, either. According to Catlett: "We have to include [boredom] because that's one of the obstacles to participation."

That also proved an obstacle for at least one critic. Writing for the *Village Voice*, Miriam Felton-Dansky bemoaned the cumulative effect of stage tedium, which was apparently "too-real"-istic.

Deliberate boredom can be artistically powerful, but here, the artists' attention to format over content – meeting routines, not narratives – backfires, leaving us less ready to care when, eventually, real high school students take the stage to tell us about disturbing changes to standardized testing in our own city. [*VV,* May 15, 2013]

Conversely, *Houston Free Press* critic John Plueker experienced the kind of cognitive dissonance that's vital to the process of political change and reflects more positively the co-creators' intentions.

I left the performance with a weird mix of exhilaration and frustration at this clash of the worlds of local politics with the demimonde of art and performance. Especially since the performance was just as messy, awkward, tense, tedious, enraging, dramatic and complicated as day-to-day life in our circa 2012, post-everything society. [*HFP*, Nov. 2, 2012]

Pieces like *City Council Meeting* take a step further than the docu-dramatist's process of adapting spoken text for performance. Like Emily Mann in *Execution of Justice* and Anna Deavere Smith in *Fires in the* Mirror, the co-creators of *City Council Meeting* researched and edited text to be spoken, and then structured an event to take place with performers and observers in a theatrical setting. Though both the source material and creative process differ significantly between those docu-dramatists and the *CCM* social practice playwrights – Mann and Smith created their texts from trial transcripts and interviews they conducted, while the *CCM* co-creators based their text mostly on documents they researched and collected – the biggest difference in terms of audience experience was that the *CCM* playwrights invited the audience to participate as actors in the performance.

This project offers two unique opportunities for playwrights: invent new forms that depend upon collaboration with an audience in the performance of a play, and participate in the cultural zeitgeist by learning more about an art movement that's gaining momentum in this new century.

Workshop: Social Practice Playwriting

The goal of the Supreme Court Do-Over project is to have writers experiment with social practice playwriting as defined by Kate Taylor: "…blur the boundaries between creator and audience and encourage political engagement."

While there are countless possibilities for research, issues, and text, we begin here with transcripts of Supreme Court oral arguments because they immediately satisfy the political component of the project. The oral arguments also offer tremendous variety in constitutional issues, so writers shouldn't have any difficulty in finding cases of personal interest.

Furthermore, these legal contests are highly dramatic and theatrical events. The judges wear costumes (black robes), as do the lawyers (their best business suits). There are characters in conflict (the petitioner and respondent), and suspense: only one side will emerge victorious from this contest. The stakes are high, because the verdict will determine the nation's laws and cultural standards, so thousands if not millions of people await the outcome. The arguments themselves are feisty affairs in which justices engage lawyers in a battle of evidence, precedent, interpretation, and wit. And there's a dramatic structure with an inciting incident (the original controversy), a progression of rising conflicts (lower court hearings) that lead to a climax (the oral argument at the Supreme Court), and finally the denouement (the Opinion of the Court).

In fact, when Justice Ruth Ginsberg was asked by a member of the audience at a speaking engagement in 2013 at Glimmerglass Opera in New York if the Supreme Court was art or theatre, Ginsberg replied, "It's both, with a healthy dose of real life mixed in." [*New York Times, Aug. 18 2013*]

With the political, dramatic, and theatrical aspects of the project covered, writers can focus on the challenge of creating a structure that invites collaborative participation from an audience.

Step 1: **Research.** Transcripts of Supreme Court cases can be found on http://www.supreme-court.gov/.

Step 2: **Select.** Find a case of interest and download the transcript from the website above. Also download the research "briefs" that support each side of the argument as well as the Opinion of the Court and Dissenting Opinions.

Step 3: **Brainstorm.** How might a performance of this case – both argument and decision – involve audience participation, either by reading the transcript verbatim or commenting on it along the way? Should it be a faithful re-enactment or a revisionist deconstruction?

Step 4: **Write/Edit.** Once writers have a concept or plan for actors to collaborate with the audience, they can proceed with editing the text, which might involve additions, elisions, and spots for interjections, improvisation, or discussion. Script the overall event, note where participants might prepare by reading briefs and other background material.

Step 5: **Try it out.** Perform/participate, then discuss. How did the event blur distinctions between actor and audience? In what ways were the outcome of the event dependent upon what happened during the performance?

Step 6: **Reflect.** Consider the impact on the participants. Were their personal viewpoints challenged? Did conflicting viewpoints create an impasse or require negotiation. If the project involved deciding the case anew, did the participants arrive at the same decision as the majority Opinion of the Court, and on what principles did they base their decisions?

◆◆◆

Social Practice Play

The Case Is Submitted: Boy Scouts of America, Monmouth Council v. Dale has been performed in two versions in different settings. Students at Goucher College re-enacted the entire text (fortunately, all oral arguments are limited to one hour), and were then divided into small groups to discuss and vote on a decision. Only after the students decided the case for themselves was the Opinion of the Court shared with them.

At Mixed Blood Theatre Company in Minneapolis, five professional actors performed the following 20-minute version of the oral argument for an audience of attorneys acquiring Continuing Legal Education credit. Two actors performed the roles of the plaintiff and defense lawyers and the comments of the nine Justices (well, eight, since Clarence Thomas never speaks) were conflated into three roles for the other actors. Following the re-enactment, the attorneys analyzed the arguments and outcome of the case.

Though those two performances did not allow for improvised interjections or unscripted questions, they could have. They also might have left room for more theatrical forms of participation – songs, dance, video, and additional text. This edited twenty-minute, five-actor version awaits further adaptation for audience collaboration from social practice playwrights. So feel free to use this text to experiment with audience involvement before proceeding into new oral arguments.

The Case Is Submitted:
Boy Scouts of America, Monmouth Council v. Dale

Adapted from the Transcript of the Supreme Court Oral
Argument by Michael Bigelow Dixon

(This case was argued before the Supreme Court on April
26, 2000, and was decided on June 28, 2000. Both audio record-
ings and written transcripts of the oral argument and the Court's
decision are available at www.oyez.org.)

HERE ARE THE SUMMARY FACTS FROM THAT CASE:

The Boy Scouts of America revoked former Eagle Scout and
assistant scoutmaster James Dale's adult membership when the organization discovered that Dale was a homosexual and a gay rights
activist. In 1992, Dale filed suit against the Boy Scouts, alleging
that the Boy Scouts had violated the New Jersey statute prohibit-
ing discrimination on the basis of sexual orientation in places of
public accommodation. The Boy Scouts, a private, not-for-profit
organization, asserted that homosexual conduct was inconsistent
with the values it was attempting to instill in young people. The
New Jersey Superior Court held that New Jersey's public accommodations law was inapplicable because the Boy Scouts was not a
place of public accommodation. The court also concluded that the
Boy Scouts' First Amendment freedom of expressive association
prevented the government from forcing the Boy Scouts to accept
Dale as an adult leader. The court's Appellate Division held that
New Jersey's public accommodations law applied to the Boy
Scouts because of its broad-based membership solicitation and its
connections with various public entities, and that the Boy Scouts
violated it by revoking Dale's membership based on his homosexuality. The court rejected the Boy Scouts' federal constitutional
claims. The New Jersey Supreme Court affirmed. The court held
that application of New Jersey's public accommodations law did
not violate the Boy Scouts' First Amendment right of expressive
association because Dale's inclusion would not significantly affect

members' abilities to carry out their purpose. Furthermore, the court concluded that reinstating Dale did not compel the Boy Scouts to express any message. (www.oyez.org)

JUSTICE #1: We'll hear argument now in Number 99-699, Boy Scouts of America and Monmouth Council v. James Dale. Mr. Davidson.

MR. DAVIDSON *(Lawyer for BSA and Monmouth Council)*: Mr. Chief Justice, and may it please the Court: This case is about the freedom of a voluntary association to choose its own leaders. The New Jersey Supreme Court has held that the State and not Boy Scouting may decide who will wear the Scout leader's uniform and act as a role model of Scouting's values for a group of 10 to 15 boys in a Scout troop. Far from a business networking organization, Boy Scouting is so closely identified with traditional moral values that the phrase, he's a real Boy Scout, has entered the language.

JUSTICE #2: Do we take this case as one in which Dale was terminated because of the reasonable likelihood that he would use his position to advocate for his cause?

MR. DAVIDSON: Your Honor, Mr. Dale had created a reputation for himself by the newspaper article which appeared, and which – the reputation which would have carried into the troop meeting and affected his ability to be a role model to the youths in his troop.

JUSTICE #1: So if it were simply called to the Scouts' attention that he was a very private person, but had said to his family that he was a homosexual, that he could still be terminated?

MR. DAVIDSON: Well, as Mr. Dale alleges in his complaint and reaffirmed in his summary judgment affidavit, Scouting does not investigate the sexual orientation of applicants and only excludes those that are open about their sexual orientation.

JUSTICE #3: Well, if a Boy Scout – well, let's just keep it at troop leaders for now. If a troop leader simply said to other officials, not to the newspapers, not in any public forum anywhere, I am a homosexual, would he be excluded from his leadership position for that alone?

MR. DAVIDSON: If the – whoever heard whatever statement was made learned that the person intended to engage in homosexual conduct felt that that was an appropriate –

JUSTICE #3: That wasn't my question. I mean, you may want to elaborate on that, but if he simply says, I am a homosexual, would he be excluded from a leadership position for that?

MR. DAVIDSON: As I said in response to Justice Kennedy's question, that precise question hasn't come up. I believe that there would be the right to do that.

JUSTICE #3: But you're defending an expressive policy, and that's one of the things that's confusing. Are you saying the policy is don't ask, don't tell, or is the policy, if you are gay you are not welcome in the Boy Scouts? Which is it?

MR. DAVIDSON: The policy is not to inquire. The policy is to exclude those who are open. That's alleged in the complaint. It's not been an issue in the case. That's what Mr. Dale alleges –

JUSTICE #1: Well, I take it from what you're saying, Mr. Davidson, that perhaps the Scouts have not adopted a comprehensive policy covering every single conceivable situation that might come up.

MR. DAVIDSON: Mr. Chief Justice, the Scouts have general moral principles in the morally straight and clean requirements of the oath and law, and they have to be interpreted by Scout leaders in situations as they have come up and certainly, in the case of those who have – Mr. Dale has alleged are openly homosexual are not permitted to be Scout leaders, in furtherance of the efforts to pursue those moral values in youth.

JUSTICE #1: So you want us to decide this case without reference to the likelihood of any public advocacy? It's just not necessary for us to address this when we decide this case, in your view?

MR. DAVIDSON: Certainly not in Mr. Dale's case, who has really constantly reiterated his intention and desire to be open, and has had considerable media attention both before the case was filed and subsequently.

JUSTICE #2: When you – I'm not sure what we're talking about when we say exclusion of people who are not openly homosexual. I mean, what if someone is homosexual in the sense of having a sexual orientation in that direction but does not engage in any homosexual conduct?

MR. DAVIDSON: Well, if that person also were to take the view that the reason they didn't engage in that conduct would is that it would be morally wrong –

JUSTICE #2: Right.

MR. DAVIDSON: – and that's the view that would be communicated to youth, that case has not come up, but it's my understanding of the policy that that person would not be excluded.

JUSTICE #2: But somebody who was homosexual and celibate, but who said, in my view it isn't morally wrong, would such a person be excluded?

MR. DAVIDSON: Justice Ginsburg, I'm not sure I got the nots right in that question, but if somebody said it was morally wrong, and that they didn't engage in it but did have homosexual inclinations, I believe that that person would be eligible for leadership, as I understand the policy.

JUSTICE #2: So again you're saying it's not the status of being gay or being candid about who you are but –

MR. DAVIDSON: It's about the message that would go to youth in the program. The youth – in accordance with a desire to –

JUSTICE #3: Well, I'm – I just – I don't understand what is the Boy Scouts' policy, and I think we've all asked about that. Is it – I took it from one of your answers that it is don't ask, don't tell. Am I wrong about that?

MR. DAVIDSON: The practice is not to inquire into the sexual orientation of leaders. The policy derives out of the morally straight and clean requirements of the law.

There's formal position statements in the record attached to Mr. Rowley's affidavit that Scouting requires homosexual conduct, regards homosexual conduct as immoral and for that reason does not appoint openly homosexual persons in the role model position of Scout master.

JUSTICE #2: Does that go for cohabiters also?

MR. DAVIDSON: I'm sorry, I couldn't quite –

JUSTICE #2: People who live together, heterosexual unions but not blessed by marriage.

MR. DAVIDSON: Well, there's certainly adulterers or other people that have engaged in heterosexual behavior which Boy Scouts has not regarded as morally straight who have been excluded.

JUSTICE #2: I don't mean – just, the incidence of living together before marriage is not so uncommon these days. I didn't refer to an adulterer.

MR. DAVIDSON: Right.

JUSTICE #1: Is it fair to say, then, that anyone who is openly homosexual and whose admission, or profession of that fact would be likely to come to the attention of the Boy Scouts themselves, be excluded?

MR. DAVIDSON: That's correct, Your Honor. The boys are –

JUSTICE #1: Openly homosexual in the sense of practicing homosexuality?

MR. DAVIDSON: Well, being openly homosexual in – communicates the concept that this is okay. This is an alright lifestyle to pursue. Whether the –

JUSTICE #1: That the sexual expression of it is okay?

MR. DAVIDSON: Absent some further statement that it would be immoral to act on the impulses, in the culture in which these statements are made we talk about coming out. We don't talk about coming out as Canadian or heterosexual or anything else. This is a statement fraught with moral meaning.

JUSTICE #3: Is it – and I take it – we may have touched on this, but I take it that the position that you've just described is not stated anywhere in a Boy Scouts manual, or even a troop leader manual? This is in effect sort of

Boy Scout common law. It's determined by the council, and the council makes individual decisions, and that's the way the policy is expressed, is that correct?

MR. DAVIDSON: Well, the record shows, although the actual article is not in the record, that in the magazine sent to all adult Scouters in 1992 there was an article about the policy, so it's not a stealth policy, but the general principle of morally straight is really very, very widely known in the Scouting movement. It's –

JUSTICE #3: The general principle is, but this particular application of the Scouts' view of the principle I take it is not stated in any official manual, either the handbook for boys that the Scouts get, or a troop leader's manual, is that right?

MR. DAVIDSON: Well, in Mr. Dale's 1972 Scout master's handbook there is a reference dealing with incidence of sexual activity that might occur in a troop that speaks disapprovingly of homosexual conduct, but there's not a –

JUSTICE #3: But that's –

MR. DAVIDSON: – formal policy statement in the troop – in either of those, of the publications, nor is there anything about adultery or any other – or a number of other –

JUSTICE #3: And I – take it you've just touched on something that I think – again, I think I understand your position, but I want to be clear. I understand that the Scouts' position on this does not in any way depend on a judgment that Mr. Dale is – presents or would present an undue risk of homosexual conduct with the Scouts in his troop, is that correct? It's not a fear of conduct?

MR. DAVIDSON: Absolutely not, Your Honor. In fact, the issue of possible sexual abuse is one that's very important to Scouts. Every Scout handbook and Scout master handbook comes with an insert which is in the record at 2248 which talks about sexual abuse at some length. It never mentions the word homosexual. In fact, the only thing it says about gender is that there's a rising incidence of abuse by female adults.

JUSTICE #3: But that's not at issue here.

MR. DAVIDSON: That's –

JUSTICE #3: It's not alleged, and that's not the basis of it.

MR. DAVIDSON: – not alleged. It's not the basis of policy in any way.

JUSTICE #3: All right. Now, clarify for me, because I – it is not clear to me yet. A heterosexual male adult who wants to be a Scout leader who openly espouses the view that homosexuality is not immoral, and that it is consistent with Scout law and oath, is that person qualified for membership as a troop leader?

MR. DAVIDSON: That person could take that position in Scouting Councils to urge that a change be made, but if that – unless that person were willing to – if that person were to take that position to the youth in the program and urge it on the youth in the program, that person would not be able to continue as a Scout leader, and that's why Mr. Rice was terminated.

JUSTICE #3: Did anything happen here, other than what's in the complaint, which I take it was that Mr. Dale, sometime in the past, was a member of the Gay Alliance at a university, gave some seminars, was interviewed then, and it was in the newspaper. Then he received a letter of termination.

MR. DAVIDSON: Right. He was then and there the copresident of Rutger's Gay and Lesbian Group.

JUSTICE #3: All right, yes, but there's nothing other than that, and when you use the word open, that's what open refers to, is talking to the newspaper reporter about his previous membership in the Gay Alliance?

MR. DAVIDSON: Yes.

JUSTICE #3: May I ask one follow-up question to the one I asked before – if homosexual conduct violates the Scout code, being straight and so forth, why is it relevant whether the man is open or not?

MR. DAVIDSON: Well, in two respects. First, if nobody knows about it, it doesn't become an issue.

JUSTICE #3: But assume the Scouts find out about a person but he hasn't – he just unwittingly let them find out, not intending to.

MR. DAVIDSON: If it becomes known to the Scouts, the person would not be an appropriate role model and presumably would not be permitted to continue.

JUSTICE #3: So the policy is not limited to open gays. It's limited to all people –

MR. DAVIDSON: It's known or avowed. In practice, it has been avowed, and rather publicly avowed.

JUSTICE #3: But my case is the one where it's found out against the wishes of the person who wanted to keep it secret, and wanted not to let the boys in the Scout troop know about it, but the administration finds out about it. As I understand your position, he would be treated just like this man.

MR. DAVIDSON: Right. The right is that of Scouting to choose the moral leaders it wants for the children in the program. Mr. Chief Justice, I would like to reserve a bit of time for rebuttal.

JUSTICE #3: Very well. Mr. Wolfson, we'll hear from you.

MR. WOLFSON (Lawyer for Mr. Dale) : Mr. Chief Justice, and may it please the Court: The State of New Jersey has a neutral civil rights law of general applicability that is aimed at discriminatory practices, not expression. The law protects gay and nongay people within New Jersey against discrimination based on their sexual orientation. Although it is one of the least private public accommodations in the country, BSA is here today asking this Court to specially excuse it from compliance with that content-neutral –

JUSTICE #3: Mr. Wolfson, I suppose literally the policy of New Jersey would require the Boy Scouts to admit girls as well. I mean, that's a status based on the sex of the young woman, and presumably your position would be they'd have to take girls as well.

MR. WOLFSON: Actually, that would not follow –

JUSTICE #3: Why not?

MR. WOLFSON: – for several reasons. First of all, because –

JUSTICE #3: Isn't that a status?

MR. WOLFSON: The New Jersey law itself, Your Honor, specifically creates an exemption for those public accommodations that are reasonably restricted, in the statute's words, to single status, and therefore the statute itself recognizes that there may be instances in which an organization that is nevertheless a public accommodation does not fall within the sex proscription otherwise in the statute.

JUSTICE #3: Well, they don't have an anti-girl message, do they?

MR. WOLFSON: No, Your Honor, they do not.

JUSTICE #3: And –

MR. WOLFSON: They do not, and in fact –

JUSTICE #3: And they're saying that they do have – however they may have expressed it, they do have an anti-homosexual expression message, so I suppose in the case of the girl who wanted to be admitted their position would be weaker than it is here.

MR. WOLFSON: Well, actually, Your Honor, there's far more in the record with regard to Boy Scouts' self-identity and purposes and concepts, and perhaps their peda – excuse me – pedagogical approach, et cetera, that relates to boys, beginning with the name of the organization, right on, than there is in this record at all with regard to any effort to convey the asserted, implicit view on homosexuality that, as several questions of the Court indicated, is not reflected –

JUSTICE #2: Well, Mr. Wolfson, if we compare the antidiscrimination laws such as New Jersey has enacted with the sort of Fourteenth Amendment principles of equal protection, the – you know, we start out with people, with kind of immutable characteristics, blacks, national origin, and then presumably homosexuals are not quite the same. Supposing we would get even further. I – one of the briefs does, the City of Boston, includes in its prohibition against discrimination ex-convicts. Now, supposing New Jersey were to pass a law like that. Wouldn't the State's interest be weaker if we're talking about, say, ex-convicts being discriminated against than it would about blacks being discriminated against?

MR. WOLFSON: Well, as this Court has clearly acknowledged, for example, in the Romer case and in the Hurley case, where it talked about the legitimacy and appropriateness of State civil rights laws that include sexual orientation discrimination within the cluster of prohibited classifications, in Romer the Court –

JUSTICE #2: Well, that doesn't really answer my question at all. I asked you if the State interest would be weaker if we were talking about ex-convicts.

MR. WOLFSON: I think on this record it's difficult to answer that question, Your Honor, except that I would say that I think this Court would look to factors like, for example, the history of discrimination that has disadvantaged people according to a particular classification, and every court that is –

JUSTICE #2: People certainly haven't liked ex-cons for a long time.

(Laughter.)

MR. WOLFSON: That's correct, Your Honor, and –

JUSTICE #2: A discrete and disadvantaged minority, or hopefully a minority.

JUSTICE #3: Your answer to this line of questioning seems to suppose a dichotomy between an entity that's a public accommodation and an entity that has expressive rights. Surely there can be both.

MR. WOLFSON: Oh, absolutely, Your Honor, as the Jaycees case and others recognize.

JUSTICE #3: If that's so, then in your view a Catholic organization has to admit Jews, a Jewish organization has to admit Catholics, and you can't have – I mean, there are many.

JUSTICE #1: So if the State of New Jersey were to say our public accommodations law applies to the Knights of Columbus, B'nai B'rith, every possible organization, if they were to say that, look to that, what would we do as a matter of constitutional law?

MR. WOLFSON: The constitutional question that would be before the Court in that case, as in this case, is whether the organization has born its heavy burden of winning an excuse from compliance with the law based on its ability to show, as the Roberts and other cases make clear, a specific expressive purpose that brings its members together that is being significantly burdened by the exercise –

JUSTICE #1: I mean, is there any doubt that one of the purposes of the Boy Scouts, if not its primary purpose, is moral formation, the Scout's oath, and all that good stuff? Isn't that what you say – he's a Boy Scout, as you say.

MR. WOLFSON: Right. That's correct, Your Honor, and –

JUSTICE #1: Okay. So moral formation is. You concede that.

MR. WOLFSON: Is a –

JUSTICE #1: And they say, and I don't know why we have any power to question it if the leadership of the organization says so, that one of the elements of that moral formation is that they think that homosexuality is immoral. Now, how does that not make it an essential part of Scouting's purpose?

MR. WOLFSON: What New Jersey has prohibited, Justice Scalia, is identity-based discrimination in its membership practices. It has not limited what Boy Scouts may say. It has not limited its ability to express whatever message it wishes to express. It has not limited its ability to require that members –

JUSTICE #1: You think it does not limit the ability of the Boy Scouts to convey its message to require the Boy Scouts to have as a Scout master someone who embodies a contradiction of its message, whether the person wears a sign or not? But if the person is publicly known to be an embodiment of the – of a contradiction of its moral message, how can that not dilute the message?

MR. WOLFSON: Assuming, arguendo for your question, that they have established that is such a message and such a purpose that they wish to convey – I will assume that to answer your question, Justice Scalia – nevertheless, a human being such as Mr. Dale is not speech. A human being is certainly not speech as to a view, or as to a message, other than perhaps the message, I am who I am, I am here, and this Court has taken great –

JUSTICE #3: I don't know that our law requires that it be speech. I think our law simply prevents the State from diluting or imperiling the message that an organization wants to convey, whether the State does it by speech, or whether the State does it by dropping a bomb. It seems to me that's what's going on here.

MR. WOLFSON: Well, no. What's going on here, with respect, Justice Scalia, is that the BSA bears the obligation of showing that it needs a First Amendment shield to excuse it from this neutral law, content-neutral law.

JUSTICE #3: Well, you seem to assume in your answer – I think you assume in your answer to Justice Scalia that the Boy Scouts do have a moral message.

MR. WOLFSON: I accepted that for the arguendo, for the purposes of –

JUSTICE #3: Well –

MR. WOLFSON: – answering Justice Scalia's question.

JUSTICE #3: – who is better qualified to determine the expressive purpose and expressive content of the Boy Scouts' message, the Boy Scouts or the New Jersey courts?

MR. WOLFSON: What this Court would look to, as the New Jersey supreme court looks to, is the record as to what burden is placed on the organization's members' ability to deliver the specific expressive purpose for which they come together. That's what the right protects.

JUSTICE #1: So if this is the basis on which you prevail, what you will have succeeded in doing is inducing the Boy Scouts of America to be more openly and avowedly opposed to homosexual conduct in all of its publications. Is that what this case is all about?

MR. WOLFSON: Actually, Justice Scalia, there is most likely a reason why they have not – why they in fact concede in their own brief that they are not an antigay organization, and they do not require members and sponsors and Scout masters to inveigh against homosexuality, or to teach anything about sexual orientation –

JUSTICE #1: They –

MR. WOLFSON: – and the reason for that, Justice Scalia, is not so much that they're afraid of losing the gay people. It's that they are afraid of losing the non-gay people who, as Justice O'Connor's question pointed out, do not agree with this policy, whose charter is renewed year after year after year, despite their not sharing this moral view, or having disagreement over this, because that's not why they come into Scouting.

JUSTICE #1: I think there's a distinction between being an antigay organization and having a policy of disapproving of homosexual conduct. You don't have to have as your raison d'etre to oppose homosexuality in order to believe that it is part of your moral code that that conduct is inappropriate, and that's the position that the Boy Scouts have taken.

MR. WOLFSON: But what this Court –

JUSTICE #1: You insist that they go further and make that a prominent part of their promotion.

MR. WOLFSON: It's their burden, Justice Scalia, to show that their specific expressive purposes, not simply views they hold implicitly, but the expressive purposes of conveying any such views, are significantly burdened, and then that those outweigh the State's interest in this neutral law. The State –

JUSTICE #1: Thank you, Mr. Wolfson.

MR. WOLFSON: Thank you, Mr. Chief Justice.

JUSTICE #1: Mr. Davidson, we'll give you a minute. You don't actually have quite that much. We'll be generous.

(Laughter.)

MR. DAVIDSON: Mr. Chief Justice, we've been in litigation on this precise issue for the last 19 years and 5 days, and I would just say this, that if you have to dissect each butterfly in order to classify it, there are not going to be many butterflies left. Thank you.

JUSTICE #1: The case is submitted.

THE END

◆ ◆ ◆

Whatever you can do, or dream you can, begin it.
Boldness has genius, power, and magic in it.
Begin it now.

　　　　　　　　　– Johann Wolfgang von Goethe,
　　　Faust [A "very free translation" by John Anster]

END BY BEGINNING

Without change there is no innovation, creativity or incentive
for improvement. Those who initiate change will have a better
opportunity to manage the change that is inevitable.

　　　　　　　　　– William G. Pollard, *www.brainyquote.com*

Some playwrights benefit artistically by writing plays for or with specific theatres in mind. Usually this has more to do with the artists at those theatres than the company's aesthetic, since only a small percentage of American theatres define themselves by aesthetic. Most craft their mission statements around concepts like education, excellence, and transcendence of the human spirit. That all-encompassing approach gives artists the freedom to choose all kinds of plays, and as a result those theatres are defined by variety in what they produce – variety of culture, genre, tone, and topic. Like public libraries, those theatres put many plays on the shelf in order to serve diverse interests of the general theatre-going public.

There is a special pleasure, though, provided by theatres that dedicate themselves to a singular aesthetic, be it defined by physical expression, playwright, philosophy, or politics. By concentrating on a particular facet in the kaleidoscopic range of theatrical possibility, these companies often achieve a kind of performance virtuosity that distinguishes them as specialists in a culture of generalists.

These theatres tend to pursue aesthetics that ignore or challenge the basic tenets of realism. And by breaking away from mainstream conventions, these theatres are positioned to make bold and original contributions to the cultural *zeitgeist*. It's worth taking a look at a few such companies in the early modern and recent postmodern eras to demonstrate how the butterfly effect can function in the theatre, i.e., how a small company can create big waves by dedicating itself to excellence in a very specific aesthetic. Here are a few of my favorites.

Founded in 1897, the Grand Guignol Theatre specialized in one-act horror plays. "Guignol" means "puppet show," and in this "Grand" version, notes theatre historian Mel Gordon, "The mad behavior and violence that excite children in a normal *guignol* would be magnified for the pleasure of their parents."

By focusing on the criminal class and sociopathic characters, writes Gordon in *The Grand Guignol: Theatre of Fear and Terror,* these *rosse* ("crass") plays, as they were known,

> created havoc with the aesthetic and ironclad structural components of the well-made play. Here none of the normative values of French society – good and evil, simple 'right and wrong,' the hierarchy of one class over another – existed. Nothing *had* to happen in a *rosse* play. Any conclusion was possible.

A theatre whose very name mocks the sincerity that realism depends upon was The Ridiculous Theatrical Company founded by Charles Ludlam in 1967. As the name suggests, ridicule of social and aesthetic norms through parody, satire, and farce were key to the company's unique brand of comedy. The Ridiculous acting style was broad and self-referential, its scenery was often surrealistic, and its attitude toward issues was delightfully outrageous.

In the 21st century, many small companies follow the North star of a non-realistic aesthetic. Directed by Anne Bogart, the SITI

Company performs bricolage texts and plays by Charles Mee with virtuosic acting emboldened by training in the Viewpoints and Suzuki Method. The Ontological-Hysteric Theatre was created under the leadership of founding director Richard Foreman in 1968. Its mission is "to make work that unsettles and disorients received ideas and opens the doors for alternative models of perception, organization, and understanding." The mission of Open Eye in Minneapolis is to create "original figure theatre, animating the inanimate on an intimate scale..." (For other contemporary companies, see the listing of *Some American Theatres Producing Non-Realistic Work* in this volume's Afterwords.)

Despite the proliferation of such theatres in recent decades, incorporating playwrights into these ensemble-based companies remains a challenge. If, on the one hand, a playwright's work adheres to conventions of realism, there are scores of theatres and developmental companies dedicated to reading and considering those plays for production. On the other hand, aesthetically focused companies tend to create their own work by devising it or working with a resident writer. So if a playwright wasn't part of the original ensemble, there aren't many opportunities there.

This means, of course, a serious young playwright needs to at least consider forming or joining an upstart theatre dedicated to whatever kind of non-realistic explorations compel her or him to write. Inventing a new theatre may seem like a lot of trouble simply to get a play produced, but there are many advantages to that investment of time and collaborative effort by a writer. First, the playwright is forced to articulate what is most important about theatre in the 21st century, and that inevitably provides substantive thought and purpose to inchoate notions and longings. Also, by participating in the formation of a new theatre, the playwright is creating an artistic home, a place to explore the world and art with like-minded artists. In his *Perspective*, playwright Kirk Lynn speaks to the rewards of having co-founded the Rude Mechanicals in Austin, Texas.

The greatest challenge, however, is worldwide. Like every other aspect of American culture, the circumstances and opportunities for making theatre in the 21st century have changed drastically. As *New York Times* editorialist Thomas Friedman pointed out in his March 30, 2013 column: "My generation (baby boomers) had it easy. We got to 'find' a job. But, more than ever, our kids will have to 'invent' a job."

To discover how the next generation can prepare for that necessity in every profession, including theatre, Friedman turned to Tony Wagner, a Harvard University education specialist. "[T]he goal of education today," argued Wagner,

> should not be to make every child 'college ready' but 'innovation ready'. ... The capacity to innovate – the ability to solve problems creatively or bring new possibilities to life – and skills like critical thinking, communication and collaboration are far more important than academic knowledge. [*NYT*, March 30, 2013]

How many playwriting programs in America emphasize those qualities: creative problem-solving, innovation, collaboration? Many programs teach playwrights how to find a theatre, but the theatres most readily found develop and produce realistic plays. Emerging playwrights are thus rewarded by the profession when they steer their theatrical imaginations and narrative explorations through the narrow straits of realism.

A new program at the Juilliard School in New York exemplifies just how much the culture of art is changing in America. In 2012, Juilliard initiated an extensive program in the business of art. Titled Business Tools & Understanding Market Context, the program offers six courses and several grants that empower the artist as entrepreneur. In the Drama Division specifically, according to the Juilliard website, funding is made available for projects that help students develop "important entrepreneurial skills to match their skills as performers."

To paraphrase Pogo, we have met the future and it is us – playwrights included. Playwriting programs can no longer satisfy the demands of making theatre in the new century with dramaturgical instruction and production opportunities. Like every other artist and administrator in the American theatre, playwrights now need to become entrepreneurs. It's a daunting prospect, but its moment has arrived. The following workshops are designed to put the wheels of invention in motion.

WORKSHOP: PROJECTS AS UNIQUE AS EACH PLAYWRIGHT

Playwrights needn't start an entire theatre in order to find a form and purpose to match their talents and passions. There is a smaller scale on which to start, and this workshop encourages writers to create projects even before they write plays.

Step 1: **Brainstorm**. Working as a group, playwrights brainstorm a list of things that disappoint or infuriate them about theatre today. Write their comments on a blackboard or surface that all can see. Most likely writers will target topics such as expense, boredom, predictability, and elitism.

Step 2: **Brainstorm again**. Start a new list alongside the first. What do artists need today? The list they generate will probably include time, money, space, encouragement, access, travel, collaboration, and opportunity.

Step 3: **Brainstorm yet again**. Start a third list next to the first two. Playwrights name things they care passionately about *outside the world of theatre*. Things like family, poverty, rap music, the environment, rock climbing, animals, nutrition, medieval history – anything goes.

Step 4: **Imagine and invent.** Each playwright creates a theatre project that addresses an issue from the first list, helps artists in ways that have been identified on the second list, and focuses on a personal passion. (None of the choices need to be taken from the lists. Writers can add their own inspirations once the ideas start flowing.) The only other requirement is that their projects must involve playwriting and new plays.

Step 5: **Describe and discuss.** Writers describe their projects. Which are most exciting, which would they attend, and which would they want to join as playwrights?

WORKSHOP: DREAM IN TERMS OF GOALS, NOT PLANS

This second workshop focuses on theatres rather than projects, and it encourages playwrights to envision a new kind of theatre, one that doesn't currently exist, and one they would like to write for. Manifestos have been used to identify and solidify artistic and political movements and examples easily found on the Internet are those for the Futurists and Dadaists, as well as the Declaration of Independence. In each of those manifestos it's clear that the movement described is necessary because the status quo is either insufficient or intolerable. A good place to begin the process of imagining a new theatrical aesthetic is by declaring an end to any allegiance to realism.

Step 1: **Read.** Other manifestos you can read on-line include "the Mozilla Manifesto," Charles Mee's "Notes Toward a Manifesto," and "Steal Like an Artist" by Austin Kleon.

Step 2: **Analyze.** What is a manifesto? How does it treat the status quo? How clearly is its purpose defined? Is the author's passion evident?

Step 3: **Brainstorm.** Working together, playwrights make lists in answer to the following three questions. 1) What do they want to react against in theatre today? 2) What is their vision for a theatre in the future? (Who attends? Where is it presented? What content is prioritized? What does it look, feel, sound, and smell like? How is it made? How does the audience participate?) 3) What do they, as artists, need to do in order to make their vision a reality?

Step 4: **Write and Title.** Each playwright pens a one-page manifesto and puts a name to their vision, movement, or declaration.

Step 5: **Read and discuss.** How do these visions of theatre for the future differ from theatre today? What stands in the way of these visions being realized – and how can those obstacles be overcome? How will the envisioned theatres find an audience? Which manifesto provides a vision or movement that others would like to join?

◆ ◆ ◆

Afterwords

*Our whole way of appreciation is starting to get out of date
...The reason: we and our forebears have a different relationship
to what is being shown.*
  – Bertolt Brecht, *A Short Organum for the Theatre*

Playwrights To Follow

There are theatre professionals whose job it is to identify playwrights of interest, track their progress, and convince their theatres (or others) to produce those writers' plays. These are literary directors and directors of new play development who ensure their theatres are responsive to new voices and supportive of new ways of working. Three of the best literary artists in America have identified eight emerging playwrights whose works are distinguished by inventions and approaches that don't fit neatly within the parameters of realistic plays. Most of these playwrights are still working in the first decade of their professional careers, but the profiles make clear why they've quickly gained notoriety, received productions, and won major awards.

The profiles that follow are written by:
> *Adrien-Alice Hansel,* Literary Director,
> Studio Theatre, Washington, DC
> *Tanya Palmer,* Director of New Play Development,
> Goodman Theatre, Chicago, IL
> *Amy Wegener*, Literary Director,
> Actors Theatre of Louisville, KY

Frances Ya-Chu Cowhig

A self-proclaimed "diplo brat," Frances Ya-Chu Cowhig was born in Philadelphia but raised in Beijing, Taipei, Okinawa, and Northern Virginia. Her work reflects this international perspective, traveling the globe from China to Guantanamo to middle America and traversing more mythical landscapes as well, such as the Chinese land of the dead. Meticulously researched and deeply political, her plays generally arise out of very real and complex circumstances – such as the use of "enhanced interrogation techniques" by the U.S. Military in Guantanamo, or the exploitation of migrant workers in Chinese factories. But the plays themselves are highly imaginative, poetic, and theatrical – informed by Cowhig's interest in physical theatre (she trained at the Dell 'Arte School) and by her utterly unique voice and vision.

With *World of Extreme Happiness*, a play set in contemporary China, Cowhig set out to write a play in which a young Chinese woman could become a tragic hero. Spanning twenty years and weaving together intimate family scenes with darkly comic political satire, the play introduces the all too real struggles facing populations with few options and little power, all rendered with biting wit, a black sense of humor, and a vivid theatricality. In *Lidless*, Cowhig's best-known play, she tackles the relationship between a female interrogator at Guantanamo and a Pakistani man she interrogated. We witness the interrogation, and then the play leaps forward in time 15 years to explore the impact of the interrogator's actions on herself and her family.

In writing the play, Cowhig was drawn to the idea of exploring the impact of trauma after the fact. "As a writer," she explains "I'm more interested in the recovery process than the traumatic event itself. So far, in all that I have written, the traumatic event happens either at the very beginning of the play or right before the play opens, and the play itself is about consequences of that original event, the characters' attempts to reinvent themselves and reframe their worldviews after their previous one was ruptured by the traumatic event." This is certainly true of *401 [Gone]*, a play that takes place simultaneously in the land of the living and the land of the dead. Centered on a brother-sister relationship, the play

235

introduces us to a young Chinese-American woman, known as 21 in the script, who is grieving the death of her younger brother by suicide. Every night she recreates the circumstances of his death to try and piece together the clues of why he did it, while her brother traverses the Chinese land of the dead – a kind of mash-up of Chinese mythology and contemporary video games.

– Tanya Palmer

Jackie Sibblies Drury

Jackie Sibblies Drury's intricately layered work addresses the difficulty of knowledge and memory, and the trouble with representing history through anything but the lens of one's own (necessarily limited) cultural position. Such is the case in her funny and then devastating play, *We Are Proud to Present a Presentation About the Herero of Namibia, Formerly Known as South West Africa, From the German Sudwestafrika, Between the Years 1884-1915* – originally written as her graduate thesis at Brown University, and first produced at Victory Gardens Theater and Soho Rep. Moving between scenes denoted as "Process" or "Presentation" – though these boundaries begin to blur – this remarkable feat of metatheatre charts the failed attempt of an ensemble of well-meaning American actors (black and white) to create a piece about a little-known African genocide. But as they struggle to construct their play with only a small trove of German letters, and eventually begin to improvise, discord brews over how the story should be told, and who has the cultural authority and experience to do so. Drury problematizes the politics of her characters' very attempt to *know* and to "touch something real" as they project their own histories onto the material. As things get contentious, the play evolves from an awkward rehearsal room comedy to a deeply unsettling revelation of the human potential for brutality – and the limitations of storytelling.

A fluid movement between converging realities also characterizes Drury's more recent play, *Really Really Really Really Really*, in which the girlfriend and the mother of a conceptual artist who has disappeared sift through his work and their memories. In the playwright's words, it explores "what we try to leave behind, what we actually leave behind, and how we deal with being left." Drury's structure brings scenes from the past into the room as the two women contend with one another, creating the feeling that memories are drifting and intruding into the present moment. The play also becomes a photography session of sorts, documenting itself as it unfolds, gathering an accumulation of moments in time.

– Amy Wegener

237

Noah Haidle

Noah Haidle came to writing through reading – he discovered the plays of Thornton Wilder, Sam Shepard, Samuel Beckett and many more at the public library in his hometown of Grand Rapids, Michigan. He decided to make a study of these plays and once he'd read them, he tried to recreate them on his own. This close study of the masters gave him a structure, but the wild imagination that started to fill them was his own – and that imagination was unlocked even further when he took a playwriting class from Christopher Durang while an undergrad at Princeton. Haidle followed Durang to the prestigious Juilliard Playwriting program, and the first play he wrote there garnered the then 24-year old a number of high profile productions.

Mr. Marmalade, a darkly comic play about a preschooler whose interior life – made three dimensional onstage – holds up a mirror to what she has absorbed from the dysfunctional adults who are supposed to be protecting her. Playful and menacing, the play introduced this compelling new voice to the American theatre; it premiered at South Coast Repertory as part of their annual Pacific Playwrights Festival, and later opened off-Broadway at the Roundabout Theatre. *Mr. Marmalade* was followed by plays like *Vigils* about a woman mourning the death of her husband who relives the moments of their life together through a series of encounters with both his body and his soul – each played by a different actor – and *Saturn Returns*, which introduces us to a man at three critical points in his life, each one 28 years apart.

In his most recent play, *Smokefall*, Haidle returns to some of his early influences – namely Thornton Wilder and Samuel Beckett – to craft a story in three parts about an ordinary family struggling to make sense of the unbearable pain that life can sometimes bring. In the first part, we meet the family on the morning before the mother is about to give birth to twins. Their thoughts and actions are narrated by a character named "Footnote", who provides the context and emotional weight behind their most mundane interactions. The second act takes us inside the womb, where the twins engage in a philosophical debate about whether life is worth living, to oddly comic effect.

And in the third part we travel forward in time to discover what remnants remain of the family that we were first introduced to. Formally stylish, richly poetic and grappling with issues of life or death in a comic, sometimes profane way, Haidle's work is both an homage to the modernist playwrights who first shaped him, and a very contemporary grappling with the theatrical form and its unique ability to give our innermost thoughts and fears tangible dimension.

– Tanya Palmer

Jennifer Haley

Big philosophical and ethical questions about the relationship between the "real" and increasingly pervasive "virtual" worlds are at the heart of several of Jennifer Haley's plays, and her innovative formal techniques evoke the troubled interface between online and offline existence. In *The Nether*, which won the 2012 Susan Smith Blackburn Prize and was produced by Center Theatre Group in Los Angeles, Haley depicts a not-so-distant future in which the internet has become nearly all-immersive. A cyberdetective questions a man with pedophiliac tendencies about his creation of a server where the most perverse fantasies can be fulfilled. As the play unfolds, its procedural crime drama opens up to a journey into the virtual realm – to an idyllic Victorian house where children await patrons who'll enact dark desires. But all is not what it seems, for one young girl is actually the avatar for a grown man with a strangely tender attachment to "the Hideaway" and its creator. In scenes that move between interrogation room and vivid virtual fantasy, *The Nether* plunges into a complex consideration of the moral limits of imagination and technology, as well as the dangers of policing thought.

Haley's use of structural invention to depict the virtual world's seduction is also evident in her widely-produced horror play, *Neighborhood 3: Requisition of Doom,* which premiered at the 2008 Humana Festival. In this tale of a suburban subdivision whose teenagers are addicted to killing zombies (who increasingly look like their parents) inside an online video game, each scene is introduced by a "walkthrough" – spoken gaming instructions that set up the action and hint at the dangers ahead. Four players portray an array of teens and parents, a choice that articulates a whole neighborhood while creating composite images of families unable to connect. Mirroring the highly constructed nature of the video game with escalating tension, lines of dialogue are stacked vertically on the page:

oh my god
go inside
and lock
the door."

Haley's language moves with tense precision, generating both laughs and a palpable sense of dread – so that when the text code switches to what appears to be a more naturalistic style for the play's finale, the game's intrusion into the "real" world is complete…and fear takes on a life of its own. While Haley's work is concerned with a variety of subjects, she has often explored the changing nature of 21st century "reality" and its impact on embodied experience and human connection.

– Amy Wegener

Lucas Hnath

Lucas Hnath grew up in Orlando, Florida only minutes from Disney World, and was raised attending a charismatic megachurch – experiences he says instilled a fascination with things theatrical. In his plays, there is often an acknowledgment of the event as a fiction or carefully built construction. Players directly address the audience to set the scene, as does the ethically compromised nurse in *Death Tax*, who is cornered into a bribe by a fearful and fearsome elderly patient who longs to be kept alive (first produced in the 2012 Humana Festival at Actors Theatre of Louisville, and then at the Royal Court Theatre, among others). In a surprising shift later in the piece, the performer announces that she will become a different character. In *Isaac's Eye* (Ensemble Studio Theatre, 2013), a figure named Actor tells us that the play is filled with both facts and inventions about Isaac Newton, and that anything that's true will be written on the upstage wall. The play concerns a (true) episode wherein Newton stuck a needle into his tear duct to prove his theory about the nature of light. Hnath's work is often concerned with celebrity, and with figures who crave immortality. His *A Public Reading of an Unproduced Screenplay about the Death of Walt Disney* (Soho Rep, 2013), staged with the actors sitting at a table and with "cut to" and "fade in" directions read aloud, imagines Disney editing the scenes of his own screenplay, manipulating his story. The play's form captures Disney's obsession with controlling his legacy, and with making a perfect, self-contained world in his image.

Hnath's language is highly sculpted; words flow down the page with carefully scored pauses and repetitions. In *nightnight*, written for the 2013 Humana Festival, communications from Mission Control and tense conversations among three astronauts in space – one of whom is hiding his dangerous sleep deprivation – are punctuated by a loud tone that interrupts transmissions. This jumps the action forward, leaving thoughts meaningfully unfinished and creating a kind of pulse that underscores the whole event. Hnath's heightened, rhythmically precise speech has been described as having an incantatory effect.

– Amy Wegener

Quiara Alegría Hudes

Quiara Alegría Hudes was born in Philadelphia to a Puerto Rican mother and a Jewish father, and she grew up surrounded by both English and Spanish. While she's far more secure speaking and writing in English, the rhythms of both languages permeate her work. "I feel like in some ways my whole family is always living in translation," she says. "Like much of myself culturally, I always feel like I live between a few worlds." The ways in which these different worlds – linguistic, cultural, socio-economic – can bump up against each other, overlap, and collide often creates the structure for her plays, if not the subject itself. While much of her work takes place in and around an economically depressed area of North Philly where her mother's extended Puerto Rican family still makes their home, the style, structure, and tone of her plays are deeply informed by her musical training, an interest which was encouraged by her paternal aunt, a composer herself, and honed at Yale University where Hudes studied musical composition.

Elliot, A Soldier's Fugue was written after Hudes returned to school, this time to pursue an M.F.A. in Playwriting at Brown University under the mentorship of playwright Paula Vogel. Inspired to write about the experience of war, Hudes interviewed her cousin Elliot, a recently returned Marine who had served in Iraq, and a third generation soldier. Before she started to write, she imagined the play as a musical composition. "As I was visualizing the play," she explained, "before I even started writing it, I just imagined three characters and their lives happening, their stories happening, on top of each other. It just visually felt like a fugue to me." Structured like a Bach fugue, the play introduces us to three generations of men from the Ruiz family – all soldiers, each isolated from each other by their silence about their experience in war.

A finalist for the Pulitzer Prize in 2007, the play set Hudes on a path to create a trilogy of plays about an Iraq war veteran struggling to come to terms with the ghosts of his – and his family's – past. The two subsequent plays – *Water by the Spoonful*, which won the Pulitzer Prize in 2011, and *The Happiest Song Plays Last*—follow Elliot's story while continuing to play with

243

musical form. The structure of *Water by the Spoonful*, which jumps between Philadelphia and the virtual world of an online chat forum for recovering drug addicts, is informed by jazz, and specifically the work of John Coltrane. *The Happiest Song Plays Last*, which follows Elliot on his unlikely career trajectory as an actor playing a soldier in a movie about Iraq, draws its musical inspiration from traditional Puerto Rican folk music or *jibaro* music – a form that as Hudes describes "uses nostalgia like a goddamn machine gun." The play features a live *cuatro* player (a stringed instrument that is the official instrument of Puerto Rico) who acts as a kind of subtextual narrator, revealing the emotional core at the center of the play.

– Tanya Palmer

Branden Jacobs-Jenkins

With an undergraduate degree in anthropology and a masters in Performance Studies (as well as a childhood spent playing minor parts in his grandmother's biblical adaptations he classifies as "Euripidean—violent and scandalous"), perhaps it's inevitable that Branden Jacobs-Jenkins's plays are shrewd, smart, and more than a little wild. Grounded in his habit of social observation, Jacobs-Jenkins's plays draw from the hypnotic language and untrammeled emotionality of Tennessee Williams, the lyricism and social realism of August Wilson, Young Jean Lee's theatrical provocations, and the anti-linear dramaturgy of contemporary German plays (Jacobs-Jenkins spent a year in Germany on a Fulbright Fellowship).

Neighbors: an epic with cartoons (2010), premiered at the Public Theater's Lab series. Part family drama, part deconstructed minstrel show, and part retelling of *Iphigenia at Aulis*, the play follows an African-American classics professor, his white wife, and their daughter, and their relationships with an African-American family of actors – the Crows, all of whom play minstrel parts in blackface – who move in next door. The play alternates between naturalistic scenes with the Patterson family and minstrelsy-inspired interludes performed by the Crow family.

Jacobs-Jenkins adapted Dion Boucicault's 1859 melodrama about a doomed romance between a white man and a mixed-race woman, titled *The Octoroon: An Adaptation of The Octoroon Based on The Octoroon*. In adapting the piece, Jacobs-Jenkins wrote new scenes, radically changed some of the play's language ("gurrrrl, those are some cool-ass white people"), and staged a series of relatively open scenes in which the actors received letters from Jacobs-Jenkins, asking them to improvise answers to questions and critical quotations as themselves, not the characters they play.

Appropriate (2012) follows the Lafayettes, a white family who return to the decaying family home in Arkansas after the patriarch's death. When an unexpected artifact is found among their father's possessions, the family members confront the complications of a family who tie you to a past in its potential dysfunction as well as opportunity to reckon with the past and release it. Although the play uses a naturalistic container, it wrestles with similar ideas of inheritance, identity, and cultural amnesia. Still relatively early in his career, Jacobs-Jenkins's roots as a social scientist inform his corpus of work. Jacobs-Jenkins's plays strive to fuse emotional, social, and intellectual response. Or in his words, "I believe that thinking *is* emotional. It's how you make sense of your own mind and of the world."

– Adrien-Alice Hansel

Young Jean Lee

Young Jean Lee's plays are curious, in many senses of that word: Intellectually rigorous, restless in their probing and experiment, as well as odd and sometimes deeply unsettling. Her plays are marked by a dramaturgy of disorientation, by a near-hallucinogenic mix of brutality and sincerity, the mundane and the highly theatrical, and the mental calisthenics of encountering both in short order.

Lee was born in Korea, and was two when her family immigrated to the United States, settling in the small town of Pullman in eastern Washington State. After completing an English degree at UC Berkeley, she pursued and then abandoned a PhD in Shakespeare, moving to New York City and working with the downtown theatre troupes National Theatre of the United States (NTUSA) and Radiohole, while refining the questions and methodology she hoped to explore herself. In 2003, Lee founded Young Jean Lee's Theater Company, with whom she writes and directs her work.

Her theatre-making is essentially an experiment in personal terror; Lee begins a project by asking, "What's the last play I'd want to do?" and then figuring out how to make it. It's led to an aesthetically and thematically diverse body of work. *Songs of the dragons flying to heaven: A play about white people in love* (2006) examines a Korean-American woman's internalized and externalized self-loathing. The play features a chorus of three "Korean" women in formal Korean dress (one of whom speaks Cantonese), and a near-anonymous white couple enacting their minor relationship drama, who eventually take over the narrative center of the play. Lee based the text for her next show, *The Shipment* (2008), on feedback from her African-American cast about the roles and stereotypes they had been asked to play, and the roles they yearned to play. The result is part neo-minstrel show and part naturalistic drama. *Lear* (2010) – an investigation of grief, death, and aging – focuses on the adult children of Shakespeare's Lear in a castle as their fathers wander in a storm; Lear's daughters are played by black actors and Gloucester's sons by white actors. The play morphs into the episode of Sesame Street that dealt with the death of local grocer Mr. Hooper.

We're Gonna Die (2011) is a one-woman song cycle featuring Lee – a non-singing non-actor – singing the first songs she'd ever written and essentially standing still in an attempt to puncture her habit of aggressive theatricality. *The Untitled Feminist Show* (2012), brought together women from the theater, dance, performance art, and burlesque worlds, and had barely any text at all. ("I realized I wanted to make a show that was feminist," Lee says, "not a show about feminism. So I took out all the words.") Lee's most recent work, currently titled *Straight White Men*, is a dare to herself to see if she can write a three-act naturalistic play.

Reflecting on what unifies her work, Lee says, "There isn't a single argument in them, ever. I'm not trying to make one point. I'm trying to lay out all of the conflict that I see, present it, and have you wrestle with it on your own. Theater allows me to present information in the way that I want to."

– Adrien-Alice Hansel

SOME AMERICAN THEATRES
PRODUCING NON-REALISTIC WORK

3-Legged Dog, New York, NY
    http://www.3ldnyc.org
AXIS Company, New York, NY
    http://www.axiscompany.org
Bedlam Theatre, New York, NY
    http://www.theatrebedlam.org
Big Dance Theater, Brooklyn, NY
    http://www.bigdancetheater.org
Bread and Puppet Theater, Glover, VT
    http://breadandpuppet.org
Broom Street Theater, Madison, WI
    http://bstonline.org
Caden Manson / Big Art Group, New York, NY
    http://bigartgroup.com
Core Theatre Ensemble, Norfolk, VA
    http://coretheatreensemble.com
Curious Theatre Branch, Chicago, IL
    http://curioustheatrebranch.com
Dell'Arte Players, Blue Lake, CA
    http://www.dellarte.com
Double Edge Theatre, Ashfield, MA
    http://www.doubleedgetheatre.org
Elevator Repair Service New York, NY
    http://www.elevator.org
Force/Collision, Washington, DC
    http://www.force-collision.org
Juggerknaut Theatre Company, New York, NY
    http://www.juggernaut-theatre.org
La MaMa, E.T.C. , New York, NY
    http://lamama.org
Looking Glass Theatre, Chicago, IL
    http://lookingglasstheatre.org
Lucky Pierre, Chicago, IL

http://www.luckypierre.org
Mabou Mines, New York, NY
    http://www.maboumines.org
Mad Cat Theatre Company, Miami, FL
    http://www.madcattheatre.org
Manbites Dog Theater, Durham, NC
    http://manbitesdogtheater.org
Margolis Brown Adaptors Company, Highland, NC
    http://www.margolisbrownadaptors.org
New Paradise Laboratories, Philadelphia, PA
    http://www.newparadiselaboratories.org
New World Performance Laboratory, Akron, OH
    http://nwplab.com
Off-Leash Area, Minneapolis, MN
    http://www.offleasharea.org
Ontological-Hysteric Theater, New York, NY
    http://www.ontological.com
Open Eye Theatre, Minneapolis, MN
    http://www.openeyetheatre.org
Pacific Performance Project East, Columbia, SC
    http://p3east.com/home.html
ParaTheatrical Research, Berkeley, CA
    http://www.paratheatrical.com
Performance Space 122, Brooklyn, NY
    http://www.ps122.org
Pig Iron Theatre Company, Philadelphia, PA
    http://www.pigiron.org
Pilobolus, Washington Depot, CT
    http://www.pilobolus.com
Project SEE, Lexington, KY
    http://projectseetheatre.com
Radiohole, Brooklyn, NY
    http://www.radiohole.com
Rogue Artists Ensemble, Los Angeles, CA
    http://www.rogueartists.org
Rude Mechanicals, Austin, TX
    http://www.rudemechs.com
Single Carrot Theatre, Baltimore, MD

http://singlecarrot.com
SITI Company, New York, NY
    http://www.siti.org
Skewed Visions, Minneapolis, MN
    http://www.skewedvisions.org
Stolen Chair Theatre Company, New York, NY
    http://www.stolenchair.org
Target Margin Theater, Brooklyn, NY
    http://www.targetmargin.org
The Builders Association, New York, NY
    http://www.thebuildersassociation.org
The Catamounts, Boulder, CO
    http://www.thecatamounts.org
The Cutting Ball Theater, San Francisco, CA
    http://cuttingball.com
The Independent Eye, Sebastapol, CA
    http://www.independenteye.org
The LIDA Project, Denver, CO
    http://lida.org
The Neo-Futurists, Chicago, IL
    http://neofuturists.org
The Rachel Rosenthal Company, Los Angeles, CA
    http://www.rachelrosenthal.org
The Satori Group, Seattle, WA
    http://www.satori-group.com
The Wooster Group, New York, NY
    http://thewoostergroup.org
Undermain Theatre Company, Dallas, TX
    http://www.undermain.org
Universes, New York, NY
    http://www.universesonstage.com
Wax Factory, New York, NY
    http://www.waxfactory.org
Young Jean Lee's Theatre Company, Brooklyn, NY
    http://www.youngjeanlee.org

ABOUT THE AUTHOR

MICHAEL BIGELOW DIXON has worked as director and dramaturg on the development and production of hundreds of new plays as Literary Manager at Actors Theatre of Louisville, Literary Director at the Guthrie Theater, and Resident Director at The Playwrights' Center. He's co-edited 35 volumes of plays and criticism, and *Breaking from Realism* is his second book of playwriting workshops following *The Playwrights' Workout* (also published by Smith & Kraus). Michael has taught playwriting at the Kennedy Center, the Humana Festival of New American Plays, Inkwell Theatre, Goucher College, and Transylvania University. He's a regular contributor to *Teaching Theatre* and *Dramatics*, and has published articles in *The Dramatist*, *Dramaturgy in America*, and *Theatre Forum*.